A Clear Eye
for Branding

A Clear Eye
for Branding

Straight Talk on Today's Most

Powerful Business Concept

Tom Asacker

PARAMOUNT MARKET PUBLISHING, INC.

Published by Paramount Market Publishing, Inc.
301 South Geneva Street, Ithaca, New York 14850
www.paramountbooks.com
Printed in the United States of America

ISBN 0-9725290-8-X

10 9 8 7 6 5 4 3 2 1

A Clear Eye for is a trademark owned by Tom Asacker and used here by permission. To obtain permission to use *A Clear Eye for* with appropriate attribution, contact Paramount Market Publishing.

This book belongs to my friends and clients who have shared their feelings candidly about branding, and who have allowed me to do the same. Thank you.

Contents

"It is the theory which decides what we can observe."

Einstein

Introduction

I once read about a psychological study designed to see how people would react to flawed reasoning, even when it flew in the face of their own very sensible judgment. It was quite revealing. In the study two people, A and B, were seated on opposite sides of a dividing wall, looking at a screen. Each person was instructed to learn by trial and error how to recognize the difference between slides of healthy cells and sick cells. For each slide, they had to push one of two buttons in front of them, "Healthy" or "Sick," at which point one of two lamps, labeled "Right" and "Wrong," would light up.

Person A received true feedback, meaning that his "Right" lamp would light up when he was correct and his "Wrong" lamp would light up when he was incorrect. These people—the A's—learned to tell the difference between healthy and sick cells with a high level of accuracy. Person B's situation was quite different. His right or wrong lamps lit up based *not* on his own guesses but on Person A's guesses. He didn't know it, but he was searching for an order where none could possibly exist.

A and B were then asked to work together to establish the *rules* for determining healthy vs. sick cells. The A's told the B's what they had learned and what simple characteristics they had looked for to tell the difference. Bs' explanations, by necessity, were subtle and quite complex —and completely bogus.

Here's the amazing part. After their collaboration, all B's and nearly all A's came to believe that the *delusional* B had a much better understanding of healthy vs. sick cells. In fact, A's were impressed with B's sophisticated brilliance, and felt inferior because of the pedestrian simplicity of their assumptions. In a follow-up test, the B's showed almost no improvement, but the A's scores *dropped* because the A's had incorporated some of B's completely baseless ideas.

This study teaches us two important aspects with regards to branding or, for that matter, any business concept. First, once an explanation for something has taken hold of our minds, information that should refute that explanation may produce *not* an appropriate change of mind but rather an elaboration of the flawed explanation. It also teaches us to beware (be aware) of abstruse ideas, no matter how convincing the presentation or how brilliant the so-called expert.

What follows is a collage of conversations that I've had during the past ten years with people who have experienced some perplexing ideas and thus have struggled with thoughts of "branding." Thoughts like: *What exactly is branding? Does it apply to me and to my organization, and if so, how? Is it just for large, consumer goods manufacturers, or is it relevant to a small business, to business-to-business firms, and to nonprofits? Can a person be a brand? How about a place? Why brand? Why not?* And so on.

In *The Practice of Management*, Peter Drucker wrote, "*Because it is its purpose to create a customer, any business enterprise has two—and only these two—basic functions:*

marketing and innovation." The execution of those two functions is what I'll be referring to as "branding." The effect—in the mind of the customer—is what I'll mean by "brand." I hope the conversation in this book provides you with a much clearer-eye on this evolved and critically important business concept. And rest assured, although I'll be compelled to toss in some hyperbole of my own, I will try diligently to keep my explanations simple and accessible. Happy reading.

A Clear Eye
for Branding

One: A Brand is NOT a Logo

"Concepts, like individuals, have their histories and are just as incapable of withstanding the ravages of time as are individuals."

Søren Kierkegaard

Executive: *I think you're in my seat.*

Tom: Huh? 8C. Oh, you're right. Sorry. Let me slide over. I normally book an aisle seat. Gotta stretch the legs, you know.

No problem. Hey, don't I know you?

No, I don't think so.

Are you sure? You look like somebody.

Trust me, I'm nobody.

No, I'm sure you are. You're somebody. What's your name?

Tom. Tom Asacker.

Tom Asacker? Asacker? You're right. You're nobody.

[Tom laughs]: Thanks. I told you.

[Exec smiles] *You do a lot of traveling?*

Story of my most recent life. How about you?

Not a lot, but this is one trip I wish I could avoid.

Business trip?

You could say that. I have a meeting to discuss our organization's plans for next fiscal year.

I've been there. Have fun.

Yeah, thanks. How about you? Business?

Yes, I'm flying in to give a presentation on branding.

Branding? Do you own an ad agency?

No. I'm a writer and brand advisor. Here you go. It's a copy of my latest book.

Interesting title: A Clear Eye for Branding. So, I presume that clear eye is yours?

If you're asking me if I'm the guy with all the answers, absolutely not. My goal is simply to eliminate all of the nuance and complexity and provide a clear eye on the questions—a way of thinking about what's truly important when building a brand.

With advertising, huh?

No, not really. Although that could be one component of a successful brand.

So what's with this subtitle? C'mon. Branding is today's most powerful business concept? Don't you mean marketing concept?

Today's most powerful organizational concept

Nope. You read it right. Businesspeople are drowning in reports, data, and advice. But all of that information isn't getting them where they want to be, because they don't clearly perceive what's going on in the world around them. That's what understanding the concept of branding is about. It will force you to understand the behaviors, desires, and expectations of your audience. You'll perceive your business—and its place in the world—in a whole new way. And you'll be driven to do something to both improve it and to improve people's lives.

Right now I'd be satisfied with improving the bottom line.

Then read the book. Get a feel for the concept.

You see, I can't even appreciate you referring to branding as a concept. It doesn't seem to be a big idea to me. Isn't branding simply an exercise in differentiation through a change in logos, slogans, and design schemes?

It may have started that way, but it's a heck of a lot more than that today. Mind you, things like logos and design still have their place. But they're probably not the most relevant aspect of your brand, especially if you're interested in repeat business and referrals.

C'mon. If logos aren't relevant, then why are bikers tattooing them all over their butts?

Look, you're confusing cause with effect. People do it all the time. They think that a particular product is found everywhere because it's so *popular*, when in fact the product is popular simply because it can be found everywhere. See the difference?

So the logo is found everywhere and that's why it's popular?

For some logos maybe, like the ubiquitous smiley face. But the motorcycle logo is primarily a symbolic construct or stylized version of the *brand*. The logo didn't cause people to become loyal to it. Everything else did. The advertising, the bike designs, the store and website experience, the owners group, the events, the pricing, the long lead times. All of which created the desired effect—the strong emotional connection. The strong brand. Be careful not to confuse the signpost with the landscape.

Tell that to our pilot. Cause here we go!

Which means it's about time for the flight attendant to teach us how to fasten our seatbelts. Just in case we haven't been in an automobile since . . . say . . . 1963.

[Exec laughs]: *Good one. So back to branding. A brand is an emotional connection? I mean no disrespect, but I have to tell you that I have no feeling one-way or the other for . . .*

say . . . the brand of soap that I purchase. But I keep buying the same one.

Okay. So why?

Why what?

Why do you keep buying the same brand of soap?

Why not? It's just soap.

Why not compare the various soaps and choose the best and, if it makes sense, the cheapest?

Are you kidding? Like I have time to kill trying different brands of soap. For what? To save a few cents?

A brand choice is a feelings choice

So you *do* have a feeling about your brand of soap. You feel that it's good enough, especially considering the trade off in time and effort required to choose a different brand.

And your point is?

That every brand choice comes down to some kind of feeling. In the late 19th and early 20th centuries when brands first became important, the feeling behind the brand choice was of one of quality and consistency: "I *know what I'm getting if I buy a particular brand of soap, or grain food, or condiment. The same stuff that I purchased last time, a full package, and no dirt!"*

Fast-forward a half-century to the boom decade after World War II. In the '50s, the average grocer carried about 2,000 products, compared with the 20,000 in today's supermarket. And most of those products were heavily advertised. The more successful the brand, the more prime shelf space it occupied. So by publicizing their "unique selling propositions" or "USPs" to a fairly homogenous market on network television, companies were able to convince consumers to buy their secret brand formulas—and grocers to provide the prime shelf space—thus perpetuating this advertising-driven consumption cycle. It was a very effective method for that time.

It still seems to be working.

Not really. Think about it. Back then, if a marketer repeated his message often enough, a large number of people would actually believe it.

"Winston tastes good like a cigarette should."

How about: *"More doctors smoke Camels than any other cigarette."* That USP was broadcast during the late '40s, a few years after the establishment of the *Brand Names Foundation*. Look, as consumers we weren't very informed or bright back then and advertisers knew it. So they spent a lot of money creating *apparent* distinctions between commodities that were *not* truly distinguishable. Heck, what is "Chicken of the Sea" tuna? There's no chicken in the sea. Did they want us to believe that it was chicken . . . from the sea . . . in that can?

[Exec laughs]: *I knew it. Make the average* appear *special. That's branding for you.*

Back then it sure was. And so what happened next? Brand inertia kicked in and we started choosing what was *familiar* and *comfortable*; especially low involvement products where differences between brands were small.

Brand autopilot.

Yes. Exactly that. Psychologists say that we're all cognitive misers. We simply don't have the brainpower to deal with our infinitely complex and ever-changing environment, so we use shortcuts of automatic thinking over considered examination. Even in today's *Temptation Island* marketplace, habitual buying remains a strong phenomenon. You're probably buying the same brand of soap that your mother used to buy.

Thanks for the history lesson, and the Jerry Seinfeld humor, but you haven't answered the question: why is branding the most powerful business concept today? All you've really done is confirm my suspicion that branding is a consumer product game of manipulation and mind control through clever packaging and mega spending on advertising.

Actually, what I'm trying to do is show you where that suspicion of yours comes from. Yes, building a strong brand used to be about awareness, jingles, clever ads, gaining mindshare, tossing out features and benefits ad nauseam, but that game is pretty much over. Especially for considered purchases. Today's message-saturated, multimedia, and culturally fragmented society has changed the very concept of the word *brand*.

Because we're more informed, and opinionated and connected?

That, plus fundamental changes in commerce and consumer psychology have permanently changed the competitive landscape. The problem is one of abundance: abundance of information, abundance of ideas, abundance of technology, abundance of capital. This wealth of opportunity has resulted in too many businesses chasing too few overwhelmed and very skeptical customers.

I know we're feeling it. We find competitors popping up all over the place.

Everyone is feeling it. In the old, less complicated and challenging economy it may have made sense to pay attention to your industry and benchmark your few competitors. It used to be enough to learn and diligently apply the latest sales and marketing tactics and techniques. It used to be prudent to treat business like war and try to *kill* your competitors. But not any longer. Things are changing too quickly.

And so this is where branding comes to the rescue.

In a word, yes! But not branding as you think of it. Branding as business strategy. Branding as a framework for thinking about your reason for being. Branding as a way of continuously sensing customer desires and rapidly delivering compelling value to satisfy those desires.

Like compelling soap value? C'mon.

Okay. How about self-perception value?

How? By showing beautiful people using a particular brand of soap in print ads?

Perhaps by showing slightly idealized versions of *real* people. Ones who are truly representative of the brand's audience. But I'm thinking about connecting with something much deeper than looks. Say, with a person's aspiration to be environmentally conscious or to help those in need.

So we've come full circle to the brand as emotional connection. Touché!

Actually, I prefer to view the brand choice as a *feelings* choice.

Emotion . . . feelings . . . pure semantics.

Not really. It may be a subtle distinction, but it's an important one nonetheless. Take logos, for instance. The question, it seems to me, is not whether a choice of a logo is important. The important question to ask about the logo—about any and all aspects of your brand—is: is it *appropriate* for the feelings that I want people to conjure up? If it doesn't matter, then it doesn't matter. Simple as that. Think of your logo, of your brand, as simply the visual or sensory representation of an *invisible* meaning.

Kind of like a sign.

A sign is *less* than what it is trying to represent. A brand is a *loaded* word or symbol, which stands for *more*: all of the ideas, values, and stories that have been built into it over time. It's an abbreviated reference for the gut feeling people have about something, some group, or even someone or some place.

Gut feeling. You mean first impression?

Sometimes. But more often it's the manifestation of distilled perceptions and feelings *accumulated over time* in people's unconscious minds. Consider the Swastika. That *symbol* is found in remains from the Bronze Age and, before the Nazis appropriated it, it was *thought* to be a charm or sign of good luck. But now . . . ?

So?

People make the brand's meaning

So, let's say that you're trying to get someone to try your product or service and you don't have the time nor the money to build meaning into your brand. What do you suppose people do when they first experience your *meaningless* logo—or website, or storefront, or advertisement, or even salesperson?

Hmm.

What do *you* do?

I ask someone.

But what if there isn't anyone around to ask? At least no one you trust.

Then I decide for myself.

Exactly! You make your *own* meaning.

So let me get this straight. People are exposed to my business—my brand—by seeing something or someone.

Or hearing. Or smelling. Or even tasting or feeling.

Right. And then they think *about what it is they've sensed and decide if what I offer—our unique value proposition—is something that interests them?*

Well, you're close. In fact, you'd be dead on if this were 1950. Unfortunately that's not how people's brains work today. It's simply impossible to rationally consider all of the choices in this chaotic and overstimulated market-place—to put all of that brand information in our heads and then sort through it.

So instead . . . ?

So instead, people take a more intuitive course of action. Instead of sensing and then *thinking* about you and what you offer, they sense and then *feel* something. They engage in *interpretive* looking or sensing.

Interpretive *looking? Are you saying that they're judging us?*

In a way. Their sensory experience causes them to *feel* a certain way and *believe* certain things about you, based on their past experiences and memories. *Then* they think about those feelings and instinctively make some sort of decision. Their feelings create a sketchy mental picture of your brand and your offering and their thoughts hastily complete that picture to support *their* beliefs, *their* assumptions, *their* biases, and even their self-perceptions. They rationalize their feelings, often in their subconscious minds.

Okay. Hold on. So I look at a bar of soap on the shelf and I create the brand in my head. I don't get it.

Let's take a hypothetical example. What if a brand of soap was packaged in a tin as opposed to being wrapped in a printed, waxy paper? What feeling about the soap would you create in your mind?

That it's probably priced too high?

Exactly. Now what if you were informed that by *not* investing in advertising, the company was able to reduce its costs and price and offer you a high quality bar of soap in a tin that doubles as a soap dish. And suppose they introduced you to this new, price-competitive soap by giving out samples at your health club. How do you feel now?

I suppose I'd try it.

Of course you would. But would you continue to purchase it and repurchase it?

Good question. I don't know.

That question is more than a *good* question. It is *the* question. Now toss this into the feelings equation: suppose you could only purchase that brand of soap at a specialty store.

Game over. No way I'm going out of my way to buy a bar of soap. I'll grab whatever works off the shelf when I do my weekly shopping.

Bingo! You've heard the expression; people won't change until the pain of doing *nothing* becomes greater than the pain of changing?

Sure.

It's the same thing with a perceived benefit. It has to be greater than the comfort of the status quo. "Good enough" is your competitor, too. The brand not only has to provide better value than what's currently available, but it must also be easy to buy and easy to use. Do you see what I'm saying?

Yes, I think I'm following you on the soap example. So back to the difference between emotion and feeling.

A feeling is a value judgment

Just what you said: *"They're judging us."* Feeling is a kind of value *judgment*. You think about something and you develop a feeling of "like" or "dislike." Feelings evaluate. It's a cognitive process. Emotion, however, is stronger. It's total. There are perceptible physiological changes. It's something that grabs you. It transforms you.

Yes, but don't I want to transform people? To get them excited about my brand?

Of course you do. But your focus must always be on

their *feelings* first. Their sense-based evaluative process. The *why* behind their buy.

So to grow my brand . . . ?

Increase customers' *pleasant* feelings—like discovery, fun, reward, a sense of belonging, increased self-esteem—which will condition desire. And eliminate their *unpleasant* ones—boredom, risk, pain, effort required, reduced esteem—which condition aversion. Spend time scrutinizing every sensory cue encountered by your customers so that the mental picture that *they* create about your offering—their sense-based belief—is the accurate one.

But what about the soap-in-the-tin example? Didn't they get the mental picture right?

Not for you. You were unwilling to go out of your way to purchase the brand. The feelings you got back from the brand—*"Wow! I get a deal. I get a free soap dish."*—were not strong enough for you to make a special trip.

I see. I think.

Let me ask you. What do *you* think makes a brand strong?

Being well known, I suppose.

Which means *what*?

Well-known does not mean strong

That when someone has a need they think first of that brand.

Okay, let's try it. When I say *rental car*, what's the first company that comes to your mind?

Okay, I'm thinking of one. So what's your point?

Stick with me and really think about what I'm about to tell you. Whatever that brand is that you're thinking of, is that the brand that *you* choose *all* of the time?

No. Why?

Because to you, that "top of mind" rental car company is *not* a strong brand. A strong brand evokes one or more of the following three behavioral attributes: you'll pay a premium for it when compared to alternative solutions; you'll go out of your way to get it—it becomes a destination in its own right; or you'll continuously repurchase it. You won't accept a substitute, within reason, of course.

What about recommending it?

Well, if you won't do any of the first three things, you surely won't recommend it. Right? Unless, of course, you've being bribed or threatened, or if it were a transactional purchase—a one time deal. Let me ask you a different question. Do you frequent any local businesses during work hours; say a particular store or restaurant?

Sure.

Well, let's say *your* place of business was suddenly relocated a few miles away from where it is now, would you continue to frequent those places?

You mean if I had to drive instead of walk, would I? Probably not to all of them.

But there are ones that you would drive back to. So ask yourself why? My guess is that it has something to do with the social connections that you've made. Or you've been conditioned to believe that you're receiving great value. Right? You probably have *no* idea, nor do you care, how the prices truly compare with the place down the street. You're going back for the feeling of belonging or of getting a good deal.

Which makes those brands strong to me. I get it. What do you think are some strong brands?

I have my favorites, but you don't need me to name them. And anyway, my brands may not ring true to you. You just thought of a few. Think of some more. Ones you're willing to drive out of your way to get to, without even considering whether or not you're getting the best price. Or ask yourself: what brands am I willing to pay a premium for or to continuously repurchase?

Or just grab a copy of the Fortune 500. All of those companies have, at one point or another, figured out the brand/feelings equation. In fact, that's how each one of them got their start. But things are changing at a pill-popping rate in today's marketplace. People's preferences are changing rapidly, which turns today's peacock into tomorrow's feather duster. And that's why branding is today's most powerful business concept.

Because the brand becomes a reference point for people? It becomes a kind of short hand for their decision-making?

Perhaps at one time, but not so much any longer. Because the more brands there are, the less they mean. If everything is a message, then nothing is a message. Right? Plus, a brand no longer has one simple meaning. The meaning is multifaceted and fluid. Remember, the brand is created in other people's heads and hearts from their past experiences and memories. And since the world of their experiences is changing rapidly—due to changes in technology, new products and services, new information, fashion trends, media influence, news reports, even relocation—their assumptions, thoughts and beliefs all change as well. Which may, in turn, affect their thoughts of your brand—your value to them. Companies don't go down from one fatal deathblow. They die from a thousand little marketplace cuts.

That's absurd. How is anyone supposed to keep up with all of those changes?

Listen, I'm not saying that you shouldn't make *some* assumptions. What I'm saying is that you must keep your business nimble and be constantly on the lookout for *your* audience's changing preferences. Learn to love the question. Look, you may own a very popular bagel shop, but if your customers get hooked on some no-carb diet, you had better see it coming and adjust to it. Anticipate and adapt, or die.

Like the Internet's effect on business?

Exactly. The no-carb diet may be temporary, but the Internet surely isn't. It's simply a different, albeit very powerful, form of commerce and communication. One that dramatically reduces the cost of doing business in many markets. And one that's having a profound effect on scores of industries. But that's a subject for another book.

You know, all of your examples seem to be consumer products. Do these concepts apply to business-to-business as well?

Absolutely. Think about it. Whether people are selling to corporations or corporations are selling to people, it's still people—people who are working and living in a very unstable world. Their perceptions fluctuate. So you must be highly aware of, and adjust to, the way your audience is changing and feeling. And I don't mean to change your mind every day about what your brand stands for. I mean to take a clear-eyed view of how your audience is thinking and behaving. Embed yourself in the world of your audience. Realize that beyond choosing brands for their utility, they also choose them for social and psychological reasons.

What type of social purpose could possibly be behind a business-to-business brand choice?

Remember, every brand choice says something about you to yourself, as well as to others. It may say that you're smart, successful, strong, stylish, whatever. Let's say a firm holds a high-level user group conference, or encourages design input to its new products and services through a secure website. This may appeal to a customer's desire to belong, or to feel connected and well informed. Or maybe a particular brand is endorsed by leading-edge practitioners in the field, which signals to others that the customer is *also* leading edge. There are many examples.

So branding is about discovering the why behind the buy— the feelings of the customer—and then?

And then making sure that you *stimulate* those feelings.

By providing things like a fair price, a high quality product, hassle-free service?

Much more than that! Today's customers *insist* on high quality, quick delivery and relatively low prices. And customer service is a dated, *lean-back* practice, where employees are paid, and technology is used, to be friendly, answer questions, and generally make the overall purchase experience an agreeable one. Customer *stimulation* is a *lean-forward* strategy, designed to increase both sales and profitability.

Can you give me an example?

Sure. The other day I pulled into a megastore simply and solely to pick up one item, and I ended up leaving with a bag full of stuff. Mind you, it wasn't superfluous stuff: I would have purchased it somewhere during the next few weeks. My point is that despite my original intention—get in, get my item, and get out—I ended up buying more. I was *stimulated* to buy more.

How?

In that particular case, the store understood precisely what makes customers like me tick—what happens to us while we are in their store, and how to influence our buying behavior with signage, placement, personnel, routes, etc. See, the store was my destination because of the particular item I was interested in, but while I was there the store used its displays like large advertising flyers to *stimulate* me to buy other items.

That's retail.

No, that's understanding how and why customers make decisions and strategically designing your business model to help them decide on you, and decide on *more* from you. Branding! Customer stimulation isn't simply about merchandizing or sales, although these appear to be a much-overlooked source. Customer stimulation is about everything!

Look, new products and services are appearing daily, and new technologies and new business models are popping up like weeds in a field to strategically carve out new niches in existing categories. So you must be constantly on the lookout for ways to connect with customers and "go deep" into your relationship with them and their relationship with you, each other, and with your brand. It's about *both* developing *and* stimulating the purchase of new products and services that improve people's lives. It's about new processes, new business models, new ways of thinking, new ways of seeing, and new ways of interacting. Branding is an endless game of seduction.

Sounds overwhelming.

To the contrary. It's invigorating. The more things change, the greater the opportunity. But that hardly matters because, like it or not, it's your only way forward.

This is starting to make a lot of sense to me. When I get back, I'm gonna get my marketing department working on this.

Whoa! Hold on a minute. Do you think marketing is a department? A place?

No, it's not a place. It's a bunch of people.

Really? Do you know what the purpose of marketing is?

That's a darn good question. I've been asking my marketing people that same question for months.

Two: Marketing is NOT A Place

"Life is largely a matter of expectation."

Horace

Executive: *Okay. So tell me. What's the purpose of marketing?*

Tom: Let's start with the purpose of business, which includes nonprofits as well. I like Drucker's definition: *"There is only one valid definition of business purpose: to create a customer,"* although I would probably toss "profitable" in there somewhere. Want to venture a guess at the only valid definition of marketing purpose?

Enlighten me.

To create and maintain a strong *feeling* with customers so they are mentally predisposed to continually choose and recommend *you*. And you accomplish this purpose through the strategic and continuous planning, execution and evaluation of the concept, pricing, promotion and distribution of goods, services, ideas, and events.

Precisely. And that's why I'm going to get my marketing people working on it.

Maybe. Do your marketing people have authority to decide how your employees interact with the outside world? Do they define and develop your new products and services?

No. Your point?

The same one I've been trying to make since the beginning. Marketing is about creating a strong brand—a strong *feeling*. And that feeling is created through your audience's experience with *everything* they sense about your company. The look and feel of your advertising, your website and email communications, your products and services, your billing and collections process, and especially, in most lines of business, your people. Person-to-person interaction is still, and will always be, the most powerful creator of feelings. Your most powerful brand enhancer.

And so marketing . . .

Is not a function. It's a philosophy. A philosophy of how you connect with *your* audience. In fact, "Marketing Department" may be a case of bad terminology causing bad thinking.

So what do we call it?

Perhaps the "Customer Department." It changes the emphasis from "doing to," with exploitive or wasteful activities, to "doing with and for"—creating relationships through shared information, insight, collaboration and coordination, both externally and internally. Marketers should act like executive editors of a newspaper or magazine, working to make sure that the publication —the brand—gets read, adopted and popularized.

And their focus should be on the feelings of their readers. Right?

Everyone's should be! Because branding is not a subset of marketing. Branding is strategy. Everyone in the organization should be focused on speaking to, and enhancing, the feelings of the customer.

A brand is not a promise

And this is where I'm struggling. Which feelings? How?

Have you heard the expression: *"A brand is a promise?"*

Sure.

Do you believe it?

I guess so. Why?

Then I'd like you to lend me $10,000. I *promise* I'll return it in a week.

You know I'm not going to give you ten grand. What's your point?

My point is that a brand is *not* a promise. If it were, you'd have given me the money based on my promise to return it.

How am I supposed to know that you'll return it?

How are you supposed to know that a business—a brand—will do what *it* says it will? A brand is *not* a promise, it's an *expectation*. And there's a big difference between the two, as you've just demonstrated.

An expectation of what? What they promise?

Of receiving the desired feeling.

Isn't that the same thing?

It *should* be, but it's typically not. Most organizations have little understanding of their audience's desired feeling. That's why they resort to price concessions, coupons, wasteful advertising and promotion and other profit-eroding activities. Great brands, however, are defined by a *deep* understanding of those feelings, and their people have developed a shared understanding and willingness to accept and take responsibility for both communicating and *delivering* on those expectations. And, by the way, increasing sales *and* profits while doing so.

So a brand is shorthand for "expected feelings?"

You got it! A brand is an expectation of someone or something delivering a certain *feeling* by way of an experience. The expectation is created through implicit or explicit communication, and it is either reinforced or weakened by the actual experience.

I'm following the communication part. Like the metal soap dish implicitly communicating "high price." But you lost me on the reinforced or weakened part.

It is a little confusing, isn't it? Here's how it works. Something makes you *feel* a certain way while you experience it—be it a song, a meal, a TV show, sales presentation, soap selection, an advertisement, or something else. But before you can actually experience it, you have to *choose* it. You make that choice based upon how you *expect* the experience will make you feel. Now, once you *have* experienced it, then your memory of that experience influences the expected feeling the *next time* it is time to choose. Your past thoughts have culminated in feelings, or memories, and those feelings now motivate your thoughts.

Whew! Could you walk me through a couple of examples? Use the soap example and maybe something a little more complex.

Sure. So, you're pushing a cart around the supermarket, checking off items on your list. You get to bath products and head down the aisle and, as you approach *your* brand of soap, you see a competitive brand of soap on sale. What do you do?

We've discussed this already. I'm not changing soap brands to save a few cents.

To do nothing is still a choice

So the *expected* feeling of prudence, frugality, getting a deal, or however the brand on sale was trying to appeal to you, wasn't strong enough to cause *you* to switch. Your feeling of "good enough," drove that purchase decision. That's typical for products that, for all intents and purposes, are the same. We go with what's familiar, either from prior use or from our exposure to advertising.

And what if my brand of soap was sold out?

Ahhh. Great question! How much risk is there for you in choosing a different brand?

I guess not much at all. Although, I did purchase a different brand of deodorant once and it simply wasn't as effective as my original brand.

Do you have sensitive skin? Is there some perceived risk factor that would prevent you from making an "on the spot" choice of a different brand of soap?

No, not really.

So here's what you'll probably do. You'll sense various visual cues, like packaging, soap color, and price, get a feel for the alternatives, and make a fairly *unconscious* decision. In fact, that's why the other brand of soap was running a sale. To get you to switch to them and go on autopilot with *their* brand.

Because my brand of soap may be out of stock?

Yes. Or maybe you'll try something different on impulse, for a change or for expediency. Or to save money. Look at store brands. Their quality and packaging is so good—and they know that *we* know it—that as soon as the major brand marketers launch a new product, the stores knock them off with their own, lower priced, and higher margin, version.

Okay, but that's soap. What about a more important decision?

Most purchase decisions work that way. Think about the last time you chose a computer, TV, insurance policy, movie, mortgage, accounting service, restaurant, or hotel. Did you sit down and make a comprehensive list of the features and benefits? Did you make a purely rational choice based on some kind of price/benefit calculus?

Of course not.

Right. Who has the time? So what *did* you do? You created a mental short list based primarily on what you've seen, heard, or read. Then you did a little shopping or a little research to get a "feel" for your list of alternatives. Or perhaps a salesperson paid you a visit. Either way, in the end it was largely the "feel" that motivated your sub-conscious decision.

Okay. Walk me through another decision. Say a movie choice. But also help me understand the brand as an expectation of a feeling. Okay?

Sure. Do you rent DVDs?

All the time.

So you walk into your local video rental store and encounter hundreds of choices of titles. Assuming that you're not walking in with a title in mind, what may influence your choice?

My mood. Who I'm watching it with.

Exactly. The context. And the desired feeling, not from the movie, but from the choice, is what?

Making a good choice. An appropriate one.

Right. So to receive the *expected feeling* of making a good choice, what precisely will you do?

I'll probably start by scanning the titles in the new release section.

And you're looking for . . . ?

Familiar titles. Great reviews. Familiar actors.

And the studios put all of that on the DVD covers, along

with eye-catching graphics, story lines and all, to . . . ?

To persuade me to rent it?

Well, to entice you to rent it, yes. But how?

I give up. How?

By arousing your expectation of receiving the desired feeling.

This sounds just like what I've always thought marketing was all about. I must be missing something.

Execution follows understanding

You're not missing anything. You're simply stuck in an old paradigm. Ask any businessperson what marketing is about and they'll answer with clichés about satisfying customer needs or "world class" service. Eventually they'll get around to the 4 Ps, USPs, viral and buzz marketing, and a plethora of brand distinctions like: brand promise, brand identity, brand image, brand religion, brand essence, brand personality, experience branding, emotional branding, digital branding, interactive branding, and on and on.

If leaders would get back to the basics and understand marketing for what it really is—helping customers choose you through the quality and creativity of your entire organization's communication and actions—they would behave quite differently. And they'd get much better results. Businesspeople are hung up on execution today. Change your perception—your outlook—and execution will follow naturally.

Sounds simple.

It may *sound* simple but it requires intense curiosity, as well as the intellectual ability and persuasive and diplomatic skills to get it adopted, embraced, and institutionalized. Especially in large organizations, where getting thousands of employees to change their basic assumptions about their company is no small task.

Curiosity about what?

About how people live, shop, and buy. About what, how, and why they choose what they choose. The "feeling." That's THE question, which then becomes the focus and passion of the organization.

I don't know if that's true for every purchase decision. Even you said, "most purchase decisions work that way." Aren't most b-to-b decisions simply too risky? I mean, a poor choice of toothpaste brand leaves you with little more than a bad taste in your mouth. Choose the wrong software solution and you're probably out of a job.

I agree. So then isn't "perceived risk" the feeling to focus on? Sure it is. Because what will making a bad choice tell someone about himself, and to others?

That he's not too bright.

Exactly. The brand choice becomes self-reflective. But instead of being concerned about the feelings of their audience, most companies are obsessed with their *stuff* or with trying to influence the decision with clever copy or flashy PowerPoint presentations.

Sure, but shouldn't businesspeople immerse themselves in the process that makes up the purchase decision? You know: problem recognition, search for information to evaluate alternatives . . .

Yes, I know. And *purchase, use,* and finally, *post-purchase activities.* Look. I'm not suggesting that marketers abandon Arndt's five stages. I'm trying to show you that the old days of viewing business as war, competitors as rivals, and bludgeoning people with persuasive messages until they give up are long gone. It's a much more complex environment with highly fragmented markets, multiple channels, and a huge amount of customer cynicism. To arrive at the solution requires vision. And it certainly doesn't lie with wacky websites and goofball events to create "buzz" and word-of-mouth. Customers aren't stupid. They can see the instrumentality behind that approach. Plus, just because people talk about something doesn't mean that they *want* it. Right?

But I always thought that word-of-mouth was the end point of any marketing initiative.

Word-of-mouth is not a referral

Nope. The endpoint would be profitable sales, and for people to become an advocate for the brand—to use and *recommend* what the company has to offer.

Recommendation . . . word-of-mouth. What's the difference?

Just because something is cool or funny, doesn't mean that it's relevant to someone's desires. Someone may laugh like mad at a fast food commercial and tell all of their friends about it, but never once consider eating the food. Face it, there simply are no one-size-fits-all formulas.

Here's an example. You be *me* for a moment and tell me what you would rather have as a marketer of a new business book: a flattering review in the top ten business magazines (by subscription numbers), or equally flattering word-of-mouth? Think about it.

Well, considering that those magazines reach a combined audience in the millions, I'd take the reviews.

Of course you would. How often do you tell friends about a new business book that you're reading? Not often, I'll bet. That's just not what's talked about in most people's social network, unless it's a business book club or blog site. Or unless you happen to be stuck on a plane like we are. Instead it's what? Other than the weather.

Sports, movies, politics, a TV show, breaking news, a local event or personal experience.

Precisely. Some kind of *inside* information. A societal or subcultural scoop, which makes the person sharing the news appear "in the know." Or it's a *story*, with conflict, resolution, a hero, and a moral, which then becomes a shared social experience. We're storytelling creatures by nature. If you dig deeply into any conversation, you'll discover some psychological or sociocultural foundation. And the same can be said of most purchase decisions.

Okay. Let's get you off your "soapbox" for a minute and away from movies, and how about taking a look at a considered purchase.

"Considered" based upon what? Price?

Why do you ask?

Because "considered" to one person is "requires no thought" to someone else. When I was a young boy, my uncle would trade in his year-old Cadillac and buy a brand spanking new one each year. Even though it was a substantial purchase, based on its price, he really never gave it much thought. He never "considered" that decision, it was simply something he did.

Right. I suppose a car purchase isn't much of a considered purchase to a rich guy.

My uncle wasn't rich. That car choice was a matter of *identity*. It was part of who he was. Heck, I've watched him drive past five gas stations in his new Caddy to save a handful of change. Haven't you ever done something similar? Haven't you tried to save a few dollars at lunch, and then turned right around and dropped twenty bucks chatting on your cell phone?

Sure. But that's impulse.

Not the *meal* selection. You probably went through the same process that a management team would go through when making a considered business purchase, albeit it much faster—problem recognition (hunger); search for information to evaluate alternatives (find a restaurant, read the menu and ask the waitress about the specials); purchase (order); use (eat); and post-purchase activities (complain).

Now you've lost me again. So exactly what do we focus on?

Help customers achieve

Focus on what's being *internalized* by the decisionmaker. The social and psychological factors. Because marketing is *not* about helping salespeople sell, and it's not about helping customers buy. It's about helping customers feel and achieve. It's about supporting and guiding. Spend your time helping your customers make meaningful connections around *their* passions.

Take a look at web-based auction sites. They're not selling anything. They're giant flea markets, helping users do what they could never possibly do on their own. *That* is the future of marketing. Do you see?

So if it's a business purchase of significant consequence?

Once again, it's still people making the decision. People who take things like service, quality, price, convenience, product depth, and knowledge for granted. Right?

Right.

So don't delude yourself into believing that there is an objective "best" of anything. I don't care if it's a car, a computer, or even a cup of coffee. Behavioral economics has taught us that there is a lot more involved in a purchase decision than a simple price/benefit analysis. You are *not* going to convince people with some precise and comprehensive calculus. If such a formula existed, there would only be one "best" brand in any particular category.

I suppose you're right.

So customers' ability to assess the relative value of the myriad of competitive offerings must be based on something else. Got a *feeling* for what that might be?

Okay, I'm with you. Because feelings *drive behavior. I have to tell you though, that this conversation is frustrating. It feels like circular reasoning.*

I understand, and do you know why it's frustrating for you? Because you want a formula. A recipe. You know, do X advertising. Do Y website and email promotion. Toss in a little PR, events, and gimmicks and . . . voila! Customers flock to your marketing meal. But it doesn't work that way. Imagine if I gave you a formula, say . . . that you should use the color yellow on your packaging, because the eye is attracted more easily and quickly to yellow than any other color. What would happen? Everyone would start using yellow and before you knew it, you'd be swimming in a yellow sea of sameness.

I see what you're saying.

Your ultimate business or organizational advantage lies in discovering your audience's desired *feeling*. And then once discovered, to get creative and develop consistently positive experiences so your audience can bring those expected feelings to life.

Look. Clearly, with regards to a business-to-business decision, people ultimately want to know about the experiences of others like them, and what you're going to do to ensure that they get a similar, albeit customized, experience. That's how people create their "short list," and that's how they rationalize away the inherent risk when making a decision. They want guidance, and they want to be sure that you're the best one to provide that guidance.

Why do you think so many large industrial firms are transitioning from product-based to service-based business models? Because that's what people value. Customers are drowning in information and screaming for help. That's where the opportunity and the profits lie.

And the same goes for consumer products?

Absolutely. In our postmodern society, everyone is free to be the authors of their own lives. What they really want is help with writing their stories.

C'mon, business isn't psychotherapy. It's Quid Pro Quo.

I agree. Something for something. *"I'll help you get the feelings that you desire, if you'll support my business or organization—my brand!"*

Sounds like a pretty instrumental mission to me.

Mission? Now there's a horse of an entirely different color.

Huh? Hold that thought. The fasten seatbelt sign is finally off and I need to stretch my legs.

Three: A Mission is NOT A Strategy

"Leaders establish the vision for the future and set the strategy for getting there."

John P. Kotter

Tom: Welcome back.

Executive: *Thanks. Now back to your comment. What's a horse of a different color?*

Mission. Please don't confuse it with strategy. Okay?

I don't think I'm following you.

Well, let's say that your mission is to feed the hungry. How do you intend to achieve that mission? What has to happen and who has to do it? My guess it that you'll need financial support of some kind. Right?

Sure. Or donations of food or time.

So where will the money or resources come from?

I suppose from donors and volunteers.

Okay. And to inspire those people to support your mission, you're going to focus on . . . ?

Communicating the problem. And the need, I suppose.

Really? I used to think that way too. Let me tell you a little story. Years ago I owned a medical device company. Our mission was to help improve the lives of people who suffered from a range of respiratory disorders through the development of innovative products. In order to accomplish our mission, we had to appeal to the network of people who served those patients—physicians, nurses, hospital administrators, insurance companies, government agencies, home healthcare providers, you name it.

A complex sale.

To say the least. But here's my point. We tried to appeal to those people by tugging on their heartstrings, or as some would say, through *emotional* branding. We were *mission-driven,* in our marketing, advertising, sales, in everything. And it was a huge waste of time and money.

How can that be? Weren't their missions the same as yours?

It had nothing to do with their missions. Of course their mission was the same: to improve patient care. But their desired *feelings*—their expectations of a new product —were much different. Those feelings included things like reducing costs, simplicity of set up and use, ease of cleaning and disposal, and so on. In addition, a complex web of relationships existed among the people in that network. And so long as we appealed to them with *our* mission instead of with *their* feelings, we struggled. Trust me. Being mission-driven is a sure way to inhibit your organization's growth. Instead, be *purpose*-driven.

And that purpose should be to appeal to our audience's feelings. To understand their priorities and aspirations. Right?

Design determines results

Exactly! What they value, as well as their fears, anxieties, and pains. And especially their desire to belong and to make meaning with the exchange of their money or time. Now don't get me wrong. I'm all for having a clear and compelling mission or cause. One that inspires employees and volunteers and engages customers and donors. But being *driven* by one's mission—whether it's to safeguard the planet, protect the inherent rights of animals, or educate our youth—is an inside-out strategy that is designed to fail.

I'm not sure I'm following you.

Ask yourself, and really think about it: *Is my organization producing the growth in customers, members, revenues, donations, etc. that it is designed to produce?*

Like it or not your answer has to be *"yes,"* because the design determines the results. So, instead of blaming the economy or the competition or trying to change people's behavior, change the design. And you can start by accepting the realities of the marketplace and transforming your organization's mindset and activities from inside-out and mission-driven, to outside-in and feelings-driven. You have to make your mission come alive for the *benefit* of your customers and members.

So what should we do with our mission statement?

Mission *statement*? I'd probably burn it. You don't need it. Because if it's not simple and compelling enough for everyone to have it committed to memory, then it's not worth the paper, plaque, wall hanging, or desk ornament that it's printed or stamped on. Do you know that I've actually seen software used to generate mission statements.

I hate to say it, but I've fooled around with a few online versions.

Madness. Again, no matter what your mission is as an organization, you must *uniquely* make it come to life for *your* customers and *your* employees. Drucker put it best, once again, when he said that the purpose of an enterprise is to *"create a satisfied customer and deliver all of the parts of the enterprise in the service of the customer."*

It's not about fulfilling a mission, making sales, garnering donations, or even making profits. Those will come naturally when you create customers and keep them motivated to return and to bring their friends. It's about being other-focused and making the discovery and fulfillment of your customers' desires part of everyone's daily work routine: from conversations around the water cooler to meetings, presentations, and even quality improvement activities. *Branding* must become everyone's job!

You know, that makes a lot of sense. Do you have any other examples?

One I'll never forget. When I was running the medical device company, I visited with the president of one of today's fastest growing yogurt companies, and one that oozes its mission of advocating for organic food and more sustainable agriculture. And I'll never forget what that guy told me when I asked him if he ever donated his company's money to help support other people's causes: *"Of course,"* he answered. *"When they can show me how donating money to their cause will help me sell more yogurt."*

Sounds a little selfish. Don't you think?

At first blush, I thought so too. But not any longer. His answer was both pragmatic and *purpose*-driven. He was intimately aware that to advance his mission, he must make strategic and tactical decisions that appeal to the desires of his customers and help his company sell more yogurt. It works like this: Purpose (on-going stimulation of customer demand by appealing to their feelings) drives conversations, decisions and activity, which in turn drives growth and fuels mission attainment. Picasso had it right when he wrote: *"It has often been said that an artist should work for himself, out of love for art, so to speak, and hold success in contempt. But that is wrong! An artist needs success. Not only to live but to be able to create his art."*

What mission-inspired organizations need today is strong leadership to redirect the organization and keep people constantly focused on success: continued growth of passionately engaged customers, members, volunteers, and donors. Without a strategic obsession on the external needs and feelings of your audience, your mission will slowly bleed to death as more successful purpose-driven organizations attract away your means of support.

How about an example of a nonprofit that's doing it right?

I'll give you an example of *how* one organization got it right. And it's as plain as that yellow band on your wrist.

You mean this LIVESTRONG bracelet?

Yes. Think about it. If you sent an email to everyone in the country and asked each person to click a button and donate one dollar to support people with cancer, what do you think would happen?

Probably nothing much.

Why not?

Because it's a pretty generic appeal and everyone is asking for money or time to support some cause or another. Plus, who's going to key in all of that credit card information to donate a measly dollar. They'll give the dollar at the super-market checkout, or to the Santa Claus ringing the bell.

Makes sense. I mean, the number of public charities in this country alone have doubled in the past decade, and the number of people doing fundraising has jumped fivefold during that same time. So then why *do* you think that people will key in that information and donate the dollar if, in return, all they get to wear is a cheap rubber band around their wrists?

[Exec laughs]: *Must be a* feelings *thing.*

Go ahead and laugh, but a lot of people have jumped onto that *brand*wagon. The Lance Armstrong Foundation has sold tens of millions of those wristbands, and they're getting orders for hundreds of thousands every single day. And aside from the millions of dollars generated, the public recognition of the foundation has grown exponentially. It puzzles the daylights out of me why other organizations, especially those with long and rich histories, haven't figured out how to engage the feelings of *their* constituents like Lance has.

With rubber wristbands?

Again, you're looking for a formula. No, not with rubber wristbands, but by strengthening the bond—the brand—with the creative pursuit of engaging communications, events, services, and yes, things! Get creative.

Listen . . . we're all working our tails off. When are we supposed to find time to "get creative?"

The first rule of holes

I'm sure you've heard the definition of madness.

Yes, I know. Doing the same things over and over and expecting different results.

Exactly. And the "First Rule of Holes?"

Huh?

Holes! When you're in one, stop digging! I see it all the time. Organizations are lost, but they're making really good time. Look. The challenge for anyone in a leadership position in today's hypercompetitive marketplace is to get over one's aversion to the word "branding," and fully understand the concept. And then to make sure that your entire organization, and in particular those that have direct or indirect contact with customers, truly understand and convey the essence of your "brand" in every single word and action.

Stop spending time and money on activities that no one cares about. Follow the wisdom in that Donovan Frankenreiter song: *"If it don't matter to you, it don't matter to me."* Your new imperative is to assess and appeal to your audience's feelings—period! Feelings are the basis for all profit generating consumption in a market at the mercy of customer choice. Focus on feelings, especially the subtle ones that customers themselves cannot articulate. And if you're doing something that has *no* impact on their feelings, ask yourself: *Can we make it have an impact and how? And if not, can we eliminate the activity and save precious time and money?* Does that make sense?

And which activities do we focus on?

All of them!

All of them? All at once?

Have you ever heard of the "Broken Windows" syndrome?

I don't think so. What is it?

Years back two researchers argued that rampant crime in the city is the inevitable result of disorder. If a window in a building is broken and left unrepaired, people walking by will conclude that no one cares and that no one is in charge. One unrepaired window is an invitation to break more windows, and then lawlessness spreads outward from buildings to streets to entire communities.

I think I read something similar in Malcolm Gladwell's book, The Tipping Point, *about the Chief of Police in an inner city making sure that graffiti was kept at bay. And by doing so, the crime rate went way down.*

Right. So, can you see the parallels between broken windows and broken brands?

Not really.

A broken brand is a business that has no idea where it's going; has no way of communicating its purpose (since none exists); and therefore cannot align its activities nor inspire its people. It's in disorder. And this disorder leads to people walking around concluding that no one cares and that no one is in charge. Employees may see problems, but they stop complaining and suggesting ideas, since they're convinced management can't do anything, or won't. I read the results of a recent survey, which showed that fewer than 10 percent of employees believe their daily activities are actually related to corporate goals. Ten percent, can you imagine?

A strong brand inspires people

That's pretty hard to believe.

But easy to understand. Leaders are not connecting their organizations' purposes to the individual's sense of accomplishment, because the organization doesn't have a purpose. There may be goals and objectives and "to-dos," but there is no unifying perspective—or strong brand— that inspires people and guides their actions.

This lack of a central organizing principle becomes an open invitation for people to run around following their own self-serving agendas. And like the broken window syndrome in neighborhoods, this lawlessness ends up spreading from employee to employee and from employee to customer. Before long, the organization is hardened with passionless team members, uninspired customers, shrinking margins, layoffs, accounting scandals, Dilbert-esque cynicism. A vicious, and totally avoidable, downward spiral.

Why doesn't the leader step in and take control?

Great question. And the simple answer is that today's world of business is too complex for leaders to "take control." In the simpler days leaders acted as police and, like the police of that time, were far more integrated in the "community." They could see—or sense—signals of disorder and intervene to protect their brand. The leaders of today—like the police of today—are dealing with a much more complex environment with widely different competitive pressures, customer demands, stockholder expectations, and workforce requirements. They are struggling with the emerging global economy, the IT revolution, and the collapse of the old Industrial business paradigm.

The only way for today's leader to prevent disorderly behavior that will ultimately corrupt his or her organization is to viscerally understand and passionately communicate the organization's brand! The leader needs to communicate the brand's compelling essence, which will inspire sharing, tolerance, teamwork and innovation, and act as a filtering mechanism for new ideas. The brand's driving philosophy will create alignment and focus, and instill confidence, and give people permission to act, and bring ideas to life. Its special spirit will engage and unify people, and compel them to self-police the organization and prevent the small but unmistakable signals of impending chaos.

Where do the feelings of employees enter into all of this?

That's another great question. You do want employees to be excited and passionate in order to transfer those feelings to your customers. Right?

Certainly.

Great brands are not reasonable

Then remember that employees want to do a good job but, like customers, they also want to gain meaning from their relationship with the organization and its purpose.

So their *feelings* about the brand and how it reflects on them and their values is critical to the brand's success. You can't force them to commit or be motivated. It's highly personal. All you can do is set up the conditions for it to occur. Teach people how the brand helps people and how *they* make up the brand. There is nothing like the feeling of being part of something important that you have helped create.

Let me tell you a story about a strong brand that started to screw up its employees' "neighborhood." There's a hospital near where I live that has passionately communicated its purpose and aligned its activities around that purpose, which is to promote, advocate, and educate for wellness. Anyway, the administration was seriously considering opening a donut shop in the hospital. The reason sounded simple enough: choice exists out in the community and the hospital has well-educated employees. Let the employees make their own choice.

Sounds reasonable. I suppose that they were simply trying to make it more convenient for their people.

That's right. And it does *sound* reasonable. But great brands are *not* reasonable. They're fanatical about their purpose and the alignment of every decision and activity to support that purpose. Leaders are there to direct and inspire. I don't remember President Reagan saying, "Please, *tear down this wall.*"

What happened to the donut shop idea?

As far as I know, the idea got tabled. But the hospital lost some passionate and committed staff during that "little" neighborhood conflict. They left because they simply didn't *feel* good referring to the hospital as "their" hospital.

Then what I'm hearing you say is that it's far too complex for any one person to control all of the activities of the brand. Is that right?

The great Scottish historian Thomas Carlyle once wrote, *"Nothing is more terrible than activity without insight."* And this is especially true today, with major problems facing the world of business. We're all grappling with the problems posed by continual change, which makes it difficult to even foresee, let alone control, the near-term future. Too many leaders have taken the easy route by ignoring their brand—their strategy—and relying instead on the proverbial carrot or stick. And their people have naturally responded by going through the motions, practicing their comfortable old routines, and camouflaging problems. There are no fresh perspectives, since the culture stifles creativity and candid discussions.

And the solution?

Put the brand at the heart of the organization and make people feel that they *exist* at that heart. The leader must provide the *insight* that Carlyle was talking about, around which activities are planned and executed. Get everyone focused on the outside and talking about customers and their feelings. Stop messing up the corporate neighborhood with disorganized actions and get back to the fundamentals. Start living, communicating, training, and taking care of your brand. Rediscover your unbridled imagination and idealistic hopes and create new and preemptive benefits for your customers. And, one last thing.

What's that?

You had better get moving. Because broken windows may be easy to repair, but broken brands definitely are not. I heard someone once compare a lack of organizational focus to hitting a thick fog while driving. What happens? We tense up and slow down. We become a two-fisted driver. We turn down the music and tell people to be quiet. Right? We can't handle communication or distractions. We lean forward to get a few more inches "out there," looking for little markers to get us through the present "situation." But what happens when the fog lifts? We relax and speed up to make up for lost time. We crank up the tunes. We enjoy the ride.

Okay, let me get this straight. We should lay out all of our organization's activities and if we can't find a reason to do one, based on some kind of "feelings" analysis, we should discontinue it? Kind of like feelings-based reengineering?

All results are external

I don't care what kind of MBA euphemism you want to toss at it, but yes. Are you up for yet another piece of Peter Drucker wisdom?

Absolutely.

Drucker said that the single most important thing to remember about any enterprise is that there are no results inside its walls. The results of a business are satisfied customers. So you must always focus on the outside.

On our audience. Start pandering to all of their psychological insecurities and whims and such?

Whoa! Who said anything about becoming a sycophant?

A what?

A lap-dog. Someone who *simply* asks what you want and then gives it to you. Would that type of person or business appeal to you? Of course not. Where's the sense of mystery? Of surprise? We want to be around strong, authentic, engaging people. People who can bring us new insights, solutions, connections, and enjoyment. People who can inspire us. Passionate people with a strong point of view, who aren't afraid to take a few risks.

So branding is everyone's job. I have to think about this. It seems a little extreme.

Why? Strong businesses and causes have always been created by strong individuals who build strong teams around ideas that *matter*.

What you're saying is that if it's worth doing, it must be directly related to the brand. So, let's say, emptying the trash is directly related to building the brand. How?

For your particular business? I'm not sure. But consider a no-frills, low-cost airline brand. Don't you think that the pilots pitching in to help the flight crew clean up the cabin improves on-time performance, and thus people's feelings about the brand? And don't you think it's a strategic initiative?

Good point. Okay, how about, say, the shipping department?

Again, I'd have to understand the essence of *your* business and how *your* brand attracts customers. But how about this example? When Henry Ford shipped Model Ts to be built overseas, he designed the packing crates so the wood could be reused to construct car roofs and floorboards.

Wow. I've never heard that one.

You see, it's a mindset, not a department. You can innovate to improve the brand for your audience's benefit in *every* department. The people answering the phones can be trained and inspired to ask customers what needs to be improved or added. Operations, billing, legal, all of them can innovate for customers. How about a phone system that doesn't irritate customers, or flexible payment options, or rapid response to inquiries, or friendly notices of past due accounts?

Use every interaction to learn more about how to provide better value. But you must be brand-driven, not functionally driven. Think outside first, then inside, then the "numbers." Don't start with financial measures and then move to internal processes, and after that, work on how to deal with the outside. That's completely backward. But it's how most people plan and operate today.

Speaking of back, I've got to get up and walk around. But I'd really like to continue this conversation, if that's okay with you.

Four: Positioning is Passé

"Consistency is the last refuge of the unimaginative."

Oscar Wilde

Executive: So back to the brand as
strategy. *What I'm hearing you say is that an organization should focus, focus, focus, but without being too appeasing to the customer. Discover what it is that makes our organization special—our essence, our position—and then get everyone singing from the same page.*

Tom: That's the tricky part.

What is?

This whole notion of positioning. Of a brand being some kind of fixed essence that is reinforced through repetitive activities. What are your thoughts on positioning?

Well, I know that we just spent a lot of time coming up with a new positioning statement.

Is that right? It must have cost you a few bucks, too.

More than a few. A lot of us wanted to backburner the whole brand development initiative until times were a little better.

Really?

Whoa! Did I just say that?

See how easy it is to fall back into the old way of thinking about branding?

ning statement. What do you

u?

_, differentiate us from our competitors, and get
ers to feel good about us and want to choose us.

Differentiate them

Now don't shoot the messenger, but now *you* have it
backward.

Huh?

If you remember any of our conversation, please
remember this: It doesn't matter what customers think or
feel about *you* or your brand. What matters is how you
make them feel about *themselves* and their decisions in
your brand's presence.

Say that again.

What?

*It doesn't matter what people think about our organization
or our brand?*

That's right. It's all about them and their expectations,

remember? And how those expectations will make them feel about themselves. But since most organizations aren't aware of this reality, they continue to tell us all about themselves and their stuff. For example, let's say you've been away on business for a few weeks and haven't been able to frequent your favorite pub or coffee shop. What do you imagine will happen when you walk back in the door? What's your *expectation*?

They'll probably ask where I've been.

Right. They'll acknowledge that you've been missing. They may even tell you that you've been missed and that the place hasn't been the same without you. So, you'll expect *what* particular feeling when you think about returning to that "brand?"

A feeling of belonging?

Exactly that! As well as a feeling of being special. We gravitate towards—and return to—people and places and things that boost our self-esteem, and we move away from those that bring it down.

Makes sense.

But I'll bet you won't even find a *hint* of that reality in their positioning statements. Instead it's probably some egocentric position about how and why they're better than the guy across the street.

Okay, I can appreciate that for a service business, but what about a product-based business? I don't think that all products boost self-esteem, do they?

First, I'm not so sure that there is such a thing as a pure product-based business any longer. Today, there is always a critical and, in many cases, defining service or "solutions" component. I'm also not sure that the things we buy and surround ourselves with enhance our sense of worth, so much as they enhance our sense of *self*.

But you just said that we gravitate towards people and places and *things that boost our self-esteem.*

You're right. I probably should have said, "people, places and things that support our sense of self." Think about it. Even a simple walk down the grocery store aisle conjures up questions like: *Am I a good parent? Do I care about the environment? Am I a smart shopper?* There are so many options available today that we have the ability to pick and choose brands to create unique identities, all the while believing ourselves to be better than we actually are.

So we want to associate with whomever and whatever will support those beliefs. We may believe ourselves to be "in the know" in our professional lives and therefore want to acquire those things and associate with those people that help us feel that way. On weekends, however, we may be armchair quarterbacks or amateur poker players and the things and people we associate with to enhance *those* personas could be completely different. Does that make sense?

Sure.

So back to *your* positioning statement. What else did you expect it would do for you?

Provide direction and focus to our organization. We know that the market perceives us a certain way, and it's probably not the same way that we'd like to be perceived. So by creating a positioning statement, we now have consensus about how we want to be perceived, as well as how to go about quickly and clearly communicating it.

That makes sense. Kind of like an elevator pitch, which creates a quick, clear and vivid picture of who you are and what you have to offer potential customers. Not just your value, but also your distinctive advantage. Right?

Exactly.

With the ultimate goal being?

That when customers decide they're ready to buy, they think of us first.

Because you tell them that they should.

Saying it does not make it so

Not overtly. Rather by creatively communicating and eventually owning a position in our audiences' minds. It's like a memory hook that differentiates us.

Let me see if I get this straight. You developed a positioning statement—one you'll use in advertising, PR, sales presentations, on your website, etc. And this slogan or tagline will make your competitive point of difference clear and, more importantly, meaningful and memorable to your audience.

That's what I was led to believe.

And this will create brand awareness, and over time, trial, preference and referral business.

Not on it's own. Obviously we have to perform to the expectations we've created.

Ah ha!

Ah ha! what?

What you just said: The expectations that *you've* created. How? By burning your name and proposition into your audiences' minds through advertising and PR?

Well.

Listen, the meaning of your message is *not* what *you* say it is. It's what customers decide it is for themselves. Remember? The age of branding as bull horning and brainwashing is over. So stop interrupting and repeating. People have tuned-out all of the chest thumping and subtle manipulation. Think about it. If you walk into a crowded room and a few people are jumping up and down and waving their arms about or whispering mysteriously to others, you'll probably be curious about what they're up to. But when *everyone* in the room is making a spectacle of themselves, you'll cease to even notice. In fact, you'll probably be attracted to the few people who are standing quietly and confidently to the side. Or you'll be searching for a familiar and trusted face among the cacophony of messages.

But everyone seems to be talking about the importance of positioning?

Of course they are. Because they're stuck in the old, advertising-as-strategy paradigm. Do you know when the notion of positioning first appeared and why?

No. Not really.

In the early 1970s a couple of advertising guys, Jack Trout and Al Reis, wrote the seminal article on positioning, and the book that followed, to promote their agency. They posited that a brand's power lies in its ability to grab a position in the mind of the consumer. Their basic approach was *not* to create something new and different, but to manipulate the messages that were already in those minds with advertising.

Their belief was that marketing was about conflicts between corporations—not satisfying customer needs and wants, and that organizations should "brand" already existing products and business concepts—like branding a cow—by manipulating the message. "We Try Harder" wasn't a new way of structuring the Avis organization and delivering a differentiated and relevant benefit, it was a "positioning" tactic. And so was "Winston Tastes Good," "M'm M'm Good," "Let Your Fingers Do the Walking," "We Bring Good Things to Life," and other positioning statements that have not withstood the tests of time in this rapidly evolving marketplace.

You know, I've noticed a lot of organizations changing their slogans.

A brand is a process, not an entity

Watch. You're going to see a lot more. That way of thinking and operating may have been appropriate thirty years ago when product and service options were a fraction of what they are today and people were still influenced by propositions like: "Helps Build Strong Bodies Twelve Ways." But not any longer. Positioning is a dated concept. But you wouldn't believe it by listening to the experts.

I heard one brand guru say that the single most important marketing decision a company can make is what to name a brand. Now come on! The single most important marketing decision? A brand's power lies in its ability to connect emotionally through a range of associations. And those associations relate directly to the improvement the brand makes in the customers' lives through things like utility, convenience, entertainment, or social connection. If the company's offering is truly unique and relevant, the name becomes irrelevant.

Maybe.

Look, people today are much better informed, well connected and extremely hard-nosed. They've been trained to be highly skeptical of any type of marketing claim. Which makes this an era of action, not talk. People expect you to *prove* your value with new, exciting and relevant products, services and business models. We're living in a marketplace driven by creativity and innovation. The concept of branding is a much more dynamic idea. Standing still and trying to persuade people with clever advertising and image-building campaigns is a self-centered waste of time and money.

But what about getting our message out?

What about it? Whenever an organization is successful, people automatically believe that it had to do with the message—the image. But it's usually about the concept. Which means that differentiation of the communication is *not* an end in and of itself. I don't care how "popular" or clever the ad or promotion is. The overall *concept* must be highly relevant to your audience—to their feelings.

Yes, but if no one knows who we are and what we offer, everything else becomes irrelevant.

I agree. And the simple answer is that you'll have to discover *what* your audience truly cares about—a far cry from what they remember—and *how, when and where* they want to learn about it. Does that make sense?

People typically want to learn about something when they are "in the market" for it. When they're in "desire mode" or "buying mode." Focus there.

Okay, but doesn't our message—our brand position—have to be unique in order to cut through the clutter and resonate?

The more important thing is to make sure that it's highly relevant. It's like writing a novel. You may be the most creative, stirring storyteller in the world, but if your audience isn't interested in the subject matter, it's all for naught. Assuming, of course, that you're interested in selling books and not simply winning awards. Can I borrow your pen for a minute?

Sure. But I want it back. It's a Mont Blanc. [Exec smiles]

Nice pen. You think it will lower itself for a moment and write on this napkin for me? *[Tom smiles]* Take a look at this grid.

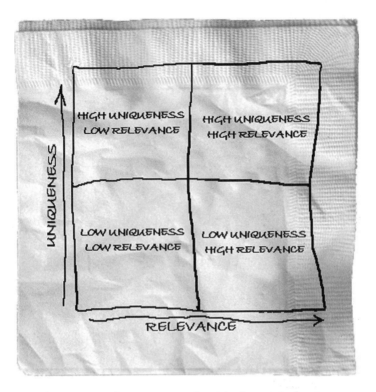

Plot your product on a graph with the vertical axis measuring your brand's level of uniqueness in the marketplace, and the horizontal axis measuring the relevance of your brand to your audience. So if you're high on the vertical axis, your brand is unique in its ability to provide something. If you're far out on the horizontal axis, people truly care about and desire that something. In the bottom left quadrant are the low uniqueness/low relevance products and services. This is where the buggy whip was located soon after Henry Ford introduced the Model T. Are there still organizations hanging on for dear life in this area? Absolutely. But we'll assume that yours isn't one of them.

Gee, thanks.

No problem. Okay, let's move up to the top left quadrant —high uniqueness/low relevance. Remember the home refrigerator with the glass door?

Sure. The see-through front that allows you to find an item before opening the door.

Right, that's a perfect example of high uniqueness and low relevance. It was definitely different, but no one wanted it. How come?

Because people didn't want to show off their messy refrigerators, I guess.

Bingo! It was irrelevant to people's desires. In fact, it made them *feel* like disorganized slobs. A lot of well-intentioned entrepreneurs waste a lot of time and money on new products, services, and communication and end up in this quadrant. So do a lot of large multinationals. The new product and new business failure rate is still well above eighty percent.

It's that high?

Absolutely. Many nonprofits occupy this space as well. Each charity or school or public service is unique in its own right, but most haven't figured out how to become highly relevant to the feelings of their audience. If they did, they wouldn't have to sweat the annual fund drive. They'd simply have an automatic withdrawal system set up with their audience.

I have that type of relationship with my online DVD rental company.

Imagine that! Okay, who do you think occupies the bottom right quadrant?

Let's see, high relevance/low uniqueness. I'd guess most businesses.

Why?

Because most offer commodity products and services that we may want, but that we can get anywhere. Or at least an acceptable substitute. Right?

A difference must make a difference

That's right. So why pay a premium or go out of your way? And it seems to me that that's why most organizations compete with coupons, discounts, loyalty cards and other types of profit-eroding activities. Unfortunately, many small and web-based businesses end up here too. They seem to be caught in some kind of time warp. Like the days of those barbershop poles spinning those mesmerizing red and white bands. They believe that if they simply set up shop and advertise, and provide good service and competitive pricing, customers will flock to them *and* keep coming back.

A "Field of Dreams" strategy. Build it and they will come.

Right. But no one ever asks: *Why should they come?* Look, the place you want to be is high and to the right—high uniqueness/high relevance. You want to be important to people's lives, to make a difference, *and* be the only one who can deliver it the way that you can. You want to continuously attract customers, and have them tell others, with something that touches a chord.

Breakthrough products.

It depends on your definition of "breakthrough." Would you consider bagged salad greens a breakthrough product?

Not really.

Of course not. It's not high-tech enough, though auto-mating the process probably was. But it was perfectly positioned in the upper right hand quadrant; it was both unique *and* relevant. It touched a chord, and look what happened. It grew into a $4 *billion* category.

You said, "Perfectly positioned." So positioning is important.

I meant positioned in the upper right quadrant. Forget

about having a unique position. Instead, uniquely *express* your position. Look at mp3 players. They're all positioned the same way. But the iPod outsells all the others combined.

I recently read a global ranking of today's top brands. Some of the biggest gainers were Apple, Amazon, Samsung, Yahoo, Goldman Sachs, Caterpillar, Motorola. Now for the life of me, I can't describe any of these brands' "position" relative to their competitors. And I'm in the "branding business."

C'mon?

I'm not kidding. I know what Apple's computer brand differentiation is, but its double-digit brand valuation growth was driven primarily by the introduction of iPod and iTunes. Can *you* tell me what they are—the "positions" those brands "own" in the minds of their audience?

You got me on that one.

I'm not trying to stump you. I'm trying to show you that growing a profitable business in today's hyper-competitive marketplace is not like what it used to be. There is no single position to own and hold on to. Try to describe the unique positions of all of the brands that *you* purchase. You won't be able to. For goodness sakes, there's a hundred-year-old automobile brand that most branding experts said would *never* be able to appeal to today's cool seekers, because of its position as a car for 60-something retirees. And today that brand is one of the most popular vehicles among athletes and entertainers.

The brand tapped into those subcultures somehow.

Exactly right. In the context of their *lives*—in music, films, video games, events—and with the look and feel of the car and the communications. People got pulled in emotionally. It required a keen and clear eye on the changing dynamics of that subculture, as well as diligence and speed in execution. The social and cultural context— the circumstances that surround the environment or situation in which your brand interacts with your audience—is a critical component of branding today.

Yes, it's important to attract people to your business and keep them coming back with promotions and experiences that they are willing to pay for and recommend to their friends. But it is equally important to stay connected to where people live—their various subcultures, like their places of business, their charities, their clubs, their pubs, their online groups, their coffee houses, their various shopping "worlds"—and to *not* rest on your brand laurels. You should assume that your formula for success up until now is simply temporary and that it will require continual adjustment and perhaps reinvention to keep up with the changing dynamics of the external environment. Have your brand be an *artist* behind all of the new ideas that touch your audience's lives, *like* a Picasso. What was Picasso's position anyway? I studied art in college and I can't seem to remember. *[Tom smiles]*

You're right. His style certainly changed radically over time.

Because he knew something that many people don't realize: success can lead to mediocrity.

Okay. So how do we define our audience—our particular subculture or "world"? Demographically?

Not any more. The beliefs and behaviors of people today have little to do with demographic or socioeconomic factors. My father was an Internet junkie at 74 years young. While in that "world," he felt comfortable, even empowered. My *younger* brother, however, is the complete opposite. He couldn't care less about the online world. I have a 50-year-old friend who's having his first child. High-income people go to dollar stores to hunt for bargains. More women are buying motorcycles than ever before. There is no "typical" anymore. People pick and choose among products, services, and experiences that allow them to feel connected, in control, and special. So choose and understand your audience based on their behaviors, beliefs, and values *while in* a particular "world" or subculture. And appeal to what most interests them—their expectations—while in that world.

And the best way to get our people to truly understand that a brand is not about cosmetics? That it's not about unaided recall or an amusing ad?

That today's audience is simply not receptive to catchy jingles or dumbed-down marketing messages? First, we must get your executives to accept the fact that creating a powerful brand is now an exercise in *strategic* differentiation. That it requires a visceral understanding of the outside world—media, technology, and culture—and the finance director's depth of knowledge of the internal workings of the organization. May I borrow your pen again?

Sure.

Go deep

Here's how business used to work. You introduced a few new products or services and then you tried to sell them to as many people as possible. You went wide. See?

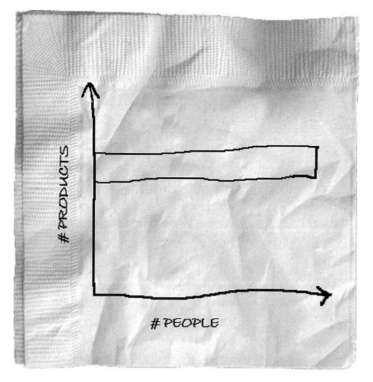

This way of operating finally produced way too many similar options and not enough time for people to evaluate and choose among them. It also tended to dilute the strength of the brand's relationship with its customers. It was simply too easy to switch to something new and better.

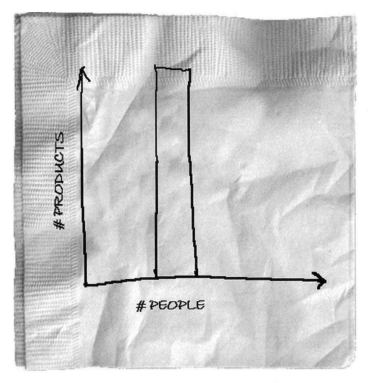

Today it's all about going deep, with relevant products and services and particularly information, into a unique subculture. Let the group define itself by its people's desires and behavior, and then introduce your brand into that subculture and get to work helping them.

Helping them do what?

Remember, we all feel uncertain about life and our choices to a large degree. So we like the brands we associate with to be confident and opinionated. To have a soul. To bring us new ideas about how to live!

Okay, but helping them do what?

Helping them do *whatever*. Save them time making a salad. That worked pretty well. Or help them with those "Now what?" moments. Remember, in the heydays of mass marketing people *wanted* to be mainstream. They aspired to be like the proverbial Joneses. Now they want to be free to create and recreate themselves with a unique combination of products, services, and associations. They want to be special *and* a part of something special. So help them do it.

It?

Whatever *it* is. Discover their half-formed concepts and unfulfilled and unexpressed wishes and desires, and help them become more of whatever it is they want to become. Whether it's more creative, more informed, more connected, more a cook, more of a biker, more of an artist, more of a parent, whatever it is. Or perhaps you can help them by freeing up some time for them or by helping them earn some extra money, so that they have more available to invest in becoming. See what I mean?

I think so.

Your brand should be like a club that your audience aspires to join. One where people can meet like-minded people. Suppose you owned a hardware store and someone walked in looking a little lost and confused. What would you ask them?

I suppose I'd ask them what they were looking for.

Not if you were in the right frame of mind. Instead, you'd ask them what they were working on—what they were trying to accomplish. Then you'd be able to engage them in a dialogue that may connect what you do—your products, services, and expertise—with what they are trying to do. Get it?

Yes, I see.

Look, times are pretty strange. People will go out of their way and pay a premium for products and services that are important to them, to their self-definition. But in categories or for things that don't matter to them emotionally, they're basically looking to save time and money. Why do you think that brand power has shifted away from the fast-moving consumer-goods companies and local merchants, to the big-box retailers?

Because of a larger selection and lower prices?

Exactly. An expectation—based on experience—of

saving time and avoiding a bad decision on stuff that simply doesn't matter much. Stuff that's "good enough."

Yes, but I've even noticed some of those retailers getting into high-end stuff. Luxury items and designer products.

And why shouldn't they? They've earned the customers' trust, and now they're going to try to go deeper into those relationships with stuff that *does* matter— whether it's aesthetically pleasing items or a range of services.

But what about the notion of "sticking to one's knitting?"

Again, I suppose it depends on your perspective. Nothing will stay the same in the marketplace. It's an ever-shifting, always evolving social institution. Why? Because exchange *creates* change. So I would suggest that one's "knitting" be as broad a range of products and services as possible, rapidly tailored to a particular sub-culture. Become a trusted source and advisor, then you can communicate with them and co-create with them how, when, and where they desire. Find as many ways as you can of gaining deeper understanding and building stronger connections with *that* audience.

And what if it's beyond our capabilities?

I would say do what those big box retailers and many online businesses are doing: outsource it. Partner up. Set up exclusive relationships with the people and organizations that want access to your audience. Business is—and always has been—about bringing people and resources together to create *change* for the benefit of customers. You either live in spirit with your audience and enhance their lives, or someone else will. It's as simple as that.

And then they'll become loyal to our brand.

Now there's a word that you can completely drop from your business lexicon.

Five: Brand Loyalty Never Was

"No more important duty can be urged upon those who are entering the great theatre of life than simple loyalty to their best convictions."

Edwin Hubbel Chapin

Executive: *What word should I get rid of . . . loyalty?*

Tom: *[Tom laughs]:* The answer to your question is yes: loyalty in business. It's a buzzword—a contradiction in terms.

You may have finally hit upon a point that I both understand and agree with. Customers are simply not as loyal as they used to be.

Now, I mean you no disrespect, but I am really tired of hearing people complain about customers being less loyal than they used to be.

Why? It's true.

C'mon. There has *never* been any such thing as loyalty to a business or organization, nor to its products or services.

I'm not sure I'm following you.

Well, consider the word "loyalty" for a moment. The dictionary says it's a feeling of allegiance and devotion. Do you really feel that those words accurately represent the "why" behind your purchase of say a brand of peanut butter or laundry detergent? Of course not. So then why have we come to believe that *repeat* customers are *loyal* customers? How have we misinterpreted historical, egocentric actions with a deep emotional bond—a bond, by the way, that's based on sacrifice, not on exchange?

In my mind what was once referred to as loyalty—back in the heyday of mass marketing—was simply habitual buying patterns and limited choice cultivated by smart marketers with mega spending on advertising and control of distribution channels. Today, those same smart marketers have added bribery to the mix. You know, *"Buy from me and I'll give you something for free!"* They call those particular tactics *Loyalty Reward Programs*.

But those tactics do *work.*

Don't get me wrong. I'm not saying that rewarding purchase behavior is a bad thing. All I'm saying is that we should call brand *loyalty* what it really is and always has been: repeat patronage. There is only one reason why people continue to associate with an organization, and that's to receive a certain feeling, or possibly to avoid one. That's it! People do *not* feel any sense of duty or obligation to an organization.

Look, I mentioned before that people are—and always have been—cognitive misers. The three pounds of gray matter between our ears can only deal with a small amount of stuff at any one time. So we are always on the lookout for ways to avoid using it. Hence, repeat purchase decisions, or non-decisions, depending on how you want to look at it.

Again, we go on autopilot.

Exactly. Think about it. If you have a son or daughter choosing a college to attend, a car making a horrible knocking sound, a boss pressing you for a detailed report, and an ill family member to care for, isn't the *last* thing on your mind going through the hassle of switching your accounts to a new bank, or reading and evaluating the labels on toothpaste tubes. Of course! So, would you call your present choice of banks and toothpaste "brand loyalty?" Of course not!

Lock-in is not commitment

Okay, but what about our organization's loyalty to, say, our software supplier?

You're baiting me, aren't you? Okay, does your organization *want* to stay with your present supplier, or does it feel that is *has* to stay, considering the cost and effort of switching?

Probably the latter.

So you're experiencing what's referred to as "lock-in" or a "switching barrier," which is certainly *not* the same thing as a committed relationship. A trapped customer is *not* a committed customer. There's a *huge* difference.

And it's a difference that's putting a lot of hurt on many small and large businesses and organizations today. And it's only going to get worse, much worse.

Why is that?

Because enlightened business leaders are using technology and other forms of innovation—including creative financing and innovative work environments that truly value people and their feelings—to make it easy for customers and employees to leave their present organization —their *brand*—and get the value they *really* desire from them.

I don't know about that. My wife is pretty darn loyal to the school where she works.

It's *not* loyalty. It's nothing more than a series of mutual concessions. The school gives your wife what she values in a work environment, including things like camaraderie, an intellectually stimulating atmosphere, fair wages and benefits, a sense of accomplishment and meaning, a convenient location, etc., and she gives them what they value. It's a reciprocal process: *Give me what I value—in a product, service, or work environment—and I'll give you what you value—money, time, intelligent work, etc. And if I decide to transact with you for a second, third, or fourth time— whether it's work for pay or money for products or services—it's simply because I expect something in return.*

Look, every organization that's in it for the long haul understands that building ongoing relationships with customers and employees increases profitability. Customers and employees become more efficient over time. They also bring other customers and employees to the organization. But despite all of this, committed business relationships are fairly nonexistent. Fickle customers shop around for the best deal, and employees job-surf because they know they're going to get caught in the next round of downsizing.

I guess that's simply the nature of the game today.

I'm not so sure that it is. Instead, we must change our mindsets. How many different ways can it be said? People don't care one bit about you or your company.

Their seemingly disloyal behavior should have given everyone a big clue. What they *do* care about is how you make them feel about themselves and their decisions in your presence. So if you want *repeat* customers, stop trying to make *yourself* feel good by ignoring their desires or by treating them in an insensitive and instrumental way, and start focusing on making *them* feel good. And maybe, just maybe, they'll come back and bring their friends.

So, I suppose we must focus on convincing them to keep coming back.

Relationships are beyond logic

Convince them? Not at all. The notion of branding as some kind of rational pursuit brimming with arguments and metrics will only distance you from people. Irresistible logic, right? *"How can you not be persuaded to choose my brand? I've proven it to you the way that one proves a theorem. Are you stupid, or what?"* This is direct marketing gone mad. You can find it on websites, in brochures, sales letters, and presentations, infomercials, you name it. You know when you come across it, because it always begins with a rhetorical question. And I probably shouldn't even refer to those types of questions as rhetorical, because they really don't enhance the persuasive effect. Stupid or manipulative comes to mind. You've read them, right? *"Do you want to lose your shirt in real estate? Would you like to save 45 percent on . . . blah, blah, blah?"*

Look, branding today can only work through ideas that customers *want* to connect with. People can neither be hypnotized with media images nor cajoled with flowery prose or "indisputable" facts. You must truly understand *their* pain, speak *their* language, and make your brand feel like a part of *their* inner world of hopes and dreams. The old world of branding was similar to an adolescent's view of love. It was about gazing into each other's eyes and being dazzled by the reflection. Today, great branding is about a mature love. It's about standing side by side in a trusting relationship with both sets of eyes focused on the horizon of life's possibilities.

Branding isn't some kind of mysterious process that only the experts can understand. It's a caring attitude and a trusting relationship. It's about mutual respect and involvement—a feeling of reciprocity. People won't believe you if you tell them they can trust you. They must *intuit* that trust, as a result of your communication and actions. So if you want customers and employees to stay with you, you have to make sure that they feel that they are gaining as much as they are giving to their relationship with you.

And we achieve this trusting, reciprocal relationship how exactly?

First, by understanding how people respond to your brand. It will typically be in one of three primary ways: compliance, identification or internalization. Compliance is the one we observe most frequently today. It describes customer behavior that is motivated by a desire to gain reward: frequent flier miles, coupons, points, discounts, free products and services. You know.

Transfer your account and get a toaster.

[Tom smiles] Exactly. Or a free safe-deposit box. So what happens? Customers typically jump around to get the best deal or to accumulate rewards, with little regard for the companies offering them. The problem with the exclusive use of this practice is that even simple organisms respond to rewards. Remove the reward and customers will stop running through the maze.

Then there's identification. *"Be like our celebrity superstar!"* Identification *is* stronger, because it's a response to wanting to be like the brand. It's different than compliance in that customers do eventually come to believe in the opinions and values of the brand, although they don't believe in them very strongly. In fact, they show very little leniency when something goes wrong. Witness the slide of those brands whose celebrities have retired or been indicted for criminal activities. Or those that were caught saying one thing privately and telling customers or employees something entirely different.

There seems to be a lot of that going on.

And there'll be a lot more, because we're living in a very transparent age with email, instant messaging, web logs, you name it. The Internet is a big dose of truth serum. Plus, the media are seeking out, and paying for, those types of stories to feed to *their* insatiable customers.

And internalization?

Internalization is the most permanent and deeply root-ed response to branding. It's what you should strive for, because the motivation to internalize a particular belief about a brand is the customer's desire to be right. It's about them—their identity *and* character, abilities, and attitude. If your brand is perceived as trustworthy—and intellectually, emotionally and socially engaging—people will accept the belief system and eventually integrate it into their *own* value system. Once it is part of their sys-tem, it becomes independent of its source and is very resistant to change. For example, if we come to believe, through deep conversations with our trusted peers, that a particular brand of motorcycle makes the very best motorcycle on the road, we too will become lifetime brand evangelists.

You're talking about my brother-in-law.

And my cousin. Look, to develop a strong brand you will probably appeal to all three. And even though com-pliance and identification are more temporary than internalization, there are circumstances that can increase their permanence. For example, permanence can result if customers discover something special about your company or product that makes it worthwhile for them to continue their behavior even *after* what attracted them in the first place—the discount or free gift or event—is no longer forthcoming.

And so enticing people to try our brand with some kind of bribe *or* bonus *isn't a bad idea after all.*

I never said that it was. And it's *not* really a bribe if your intention is to build a relationship. Is it a bribe to bring your date a bouquet of flowers?

I see what you're saying.

But remember, you *must* be prepared to grow the relationship. It's like buying dinner for someone to whom you're attracted and with whom you'd like to build a relationship. If *all* you do is continue to buy the person dinner or a drink or whatever, you'll be out of luck. She'll take your freebies, and then develop a deeper relationship with someone else. Someone who will help her validate her worldview. Someone who will introduce her to new possibilities; help her to grow.

Remember also that branding is a social science, not a physical one. There are no absolutes. Things change. New products and services are being introduced daily. New communication methods are being tested and employed.

Media influence, economic fluctuations, lifestyle and demographic changes—all affect people's perception over time. And this changes people's feelings. And their feelings about *you*.

Can you suggest any ways to stay abreast of these changes, while maintaining our audience's trust?

Marketplace trust is transactional trust

Sure, but understand that trust in a business context is a highly contingent feeling. It's about people relying on you for some future action or, to stick to our branding discussion, some future *feeling*. They intuit trust based on their expectation. And that expectation of a future feeling comes from . . . ?

What do you mean?

Where does this hypothetical person, be it a customer, employee, or prospect, get his or her expectation?

I think I see where you're heading with this. It could be through an ad, packaging, a website, a conversation with a salesperson, an experience, or word-of-mouth.

Right, and this is important because if this type of *transactional* trust is broken—if a person's expectations are not met—it's replaced by an adversarial, advantage seeking mindset. Organizations may *think* they're being smart by drawing customers in with a clever ad, but if the customer's experience doesn't match the expectation created, the organization has actually weakened its brand.

I've had it happen to me.

What?

I was attracted to a place of business based on what I heard in their ad. You know, "We love you. We're always here for you. We're fun." So I drove there and I couldn't find anyone to help me. And when I finally did find someone, he wouldn't even make genuine eye contact with me.

How did that experience make you feel?

It made me feel kind of stupid for going there in the first place.

We've all had something similar happen to us, and we detest those who play us for fools or make us feel inferior. So, what do we do? We become cynical. We *may* get even, right?

Well, I don't know about that. But I certainly won't go back or go out of my way to help them in any way.

But isn't that the same thing as getting even with them. You may see ways to save them from harm or help them to grow, but instead of pointing it out you simply let them suffer the consequences. You see, business success was much simpler, even as recently as twenty years ago. Back then it was still about beating the competition, which may have been appropriate when the playing field and the rules were fairly constant. But today, the *competitive* model has been rendered obsolete and replaced by the mutually beneficial *relationship* model—caring about the growth of the other *and* helping them grow. Why? Because things are moving much too quickly and in divergent directions for any brand to figure it all out on its own. Organizations *need* customers, not simply as a source of revenue but as a source of information, ideas, and direction.

But those types of relationships take time and patience. How does that square with the need for short-term results?

Look, you may be able to achieve your short-term *profitability* goals by eliminating the activities and expenditures that are not contributing to a trusting relationship with clients, but growth requires a long-term perspective and a collaborative mindset.

Patience.

Patience doesn't mean passive

Yes, but patience doesn't mean passively waiting for something to happen. Rather, it's a kind of participation with the customer in which you give fully of yourself.

One in which you both keep your responses, expectations, and willingness to negotiate very *open*. Have you heard of the Johari window?

Sure. We've used it internally during some teambuilding exercises to improve our interpersonal relationships.

To help you build a bond of trust *internally*. Right?

Exactly.

Well, it may also help you evaluate the kind of genuine relationship you want to develop *externally*—with customers and suppliers—by expanding your self-knowledge and modifying your behaviors to connect more deeply with them. Our society is constructed so that many of us get very specialized. We come to know only a small field, or our own business or industry very well, while being virtually ignorant of all others. This specialization is blinding many of us to what is happening in the world today.

You want the pen again, don't you?

[Tom laughs] Thanks. I get a kick out of the name: *Johari* window. It sounds like some mysterious Indian concept, when in fact it's a combination of the inventors' names—Joseph Luf (Jo) and Harry Ingham (hari).

[Exec laughs] *They had a good sense of humor.*

I think so too. Here's what it looks like, remember?

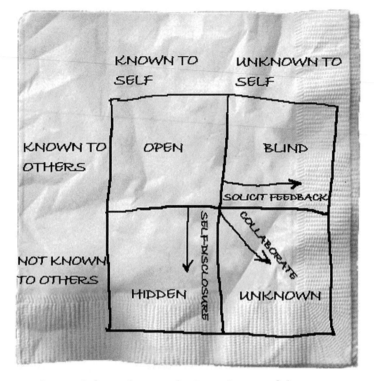

KNOWN TO SELF · UNKNOWN TO SELF

KNOWN TO OTHERS · OPEN · BLIND

SOLICIT FEEDBACK

NOT KNOWN TO OTHERS · HIDDEN · UNKNOWN

SELF-DISCLOSURE

COLLABORATE

The top left quadrant is the "open" pane of the window, which represents the information and feelings known about you—about your brand—by you *and* by your audience. The larger this pane, the better, because people tend to trust brands that are open to sharing their thoughts candidly and receiving feedback.

I remember receiving an email from the CEO of an online retailer a few years back, which explained in detail his brand's plans for testing free shipping on orders above a certain amount. What made the email a great example of openness was the conversational tone of the message and his complete and candid disclosure. He explained that the new shipping arrangement would be very expensive for the company to test and, in fact, may prove to be too expensive to continue if enough people didn't sign up for it. He also told why he was offering the new service— his brand's motivation—how long the test would run, and answered pretty much everything that his customers were probably asking themselves.

The bottom left quadrant is called the "hidden" pane because it represents the information, feelings, and capabilities that *you* know about your brand, but which you choose not to share with the outside world. These may be manipulative intentions, small exaggerations, hidden agendas, or even something that the brand considers irrelevant. It's important to weed these out, because if others sense that they are not seeing the whole picture about you and your brand it will erode their trust. So always ask yourself why? Why are we *not* telling our audience about this? Are we ashamed of something? Then let's fix it! Why are we not asking our audience's opinion on this decision?

Be transparent. Ask them for help.

Yes, *and* try to turn as much control as possible over to them. Trust is not solely a matter of credibility and transparency. You must also display a genuine *other* orientation by demonstrating your willingness to trust them and their judgment.

What do you mean by "turning control over to them?" I'm not sure I'm following you.

Do you remember hearing that people would never pump their own gas?

Sure. I'm obviously old enough.

[Tom laughs] Me too. But think about it. Today, we not only pump our own gas, we also scan and bag our own groceries, check ourselves in at the airport, trade stocks online, and customize our own financial products. You name it and it's probably being done. Customers *want* control. So give it to them. They *want* to participate. So let them. Help them organize. Then you—your brand— become an enabler, an advocate, a trusted advisor.

Yes, but don't you think that a lot of people still distrust computers and the Internet?

You tell me. What are your thoughts about selling, say, used cars over the Internet?

Used cars? It'll never happen. That has to be the least *trusted business exchange going.*

So what if I told you that over $5 billion of *used* cars were sold through online auctions last year alone?

Wow! That's incredible.

No, that's the power of creating a transparent, trusting relationship with customers. Remember the last chart I showed you about going deep versus going wide?

Sure.

Be interested, not interesting

In the days of mass marketing dominance, corporations didn't care about going deep into a relationship with customers and *opening up* with them. They did a little R&D, blasted their ads all over the place, and then curled up in isolation in the top left hand corner of the grid and relaxed. Because what ever they told us to buy, we bought. But now those same companies are struggling, because there's a wealth of choice and we're simply not persuaded by their clever marketing. Which brings me to the upper right quadrant—the "blind" pane. This quadrant represents aspects of your brand that your audience may see more clearly than *you* do. Perhaps, as an example, believing that people will not trust the Internet to do their banking.

Or my feeling about buying used cars.

Right. Now, whereas you *open up* the "hidden" area through exposure and self-disclosure, you open up the "blind" pane by developing unique ways to generate feedback, and by modeling ideas—trying new things on a small scale or trial basis. This represents a major learning opportunity waiting to be capitalized on, but it involves taking some risks as well as a willingness to put your trust in others. So reach out to your audience, and don't be afraid to ask questions.

Would the use of focus groups fit there?

Yes, but I wouldn't place much confidence in that particular method of feedback or discovery. First, there really isn't enough time for the leader of the group to develop trust with participants, so participants will probably *not* speak their true feelings. Also, since they sense that strangers are judging them, they'll have a tendency to give politically correct answers or try to appear smart, regardless of their actual intentions in the marketplace. Plus remember, many feelings that influence people's behavior occur in their subconscious minds and simply cannot be accessed and expressed in that type of forum.

That sounds right. And the lower right quadrant—the "unknown" pane?

These are things that neither you *nor* your audience knows about your brand. It represents exciting new opportunities for growth, which are discovered primarily through a collaborative process.

This all sounds pretty complex.

It really boils down to something fairly simple that we talked about earlier.

What's that?

The fact that people want you to be genuinely interested in *them*. Then they are more likely to open up and give you the information that you need to grow. They'll reveal more intimate details about their personal lives. Listen, customers are *very* smart and they really do want to be helpful. But, everyone in your organization must demonstrate respect for customers and view them as advocates, not adversaries.

Sounds like a pretty tough transition.

It may be, so start small and build on your momentum. Your simple increase in interaction with the outside world will necessarily affect a change in everyone's behavior. Start by finding out what your customers truly desire and then respond to them in a way that says, *"We understand you, because we're like you."* Let *them* define their priorities and then make sure that your people, products, and communication connect emotionally with those priorities and evoke a sense of warmth and support. And by all means, make sure to practice reciprocation in all of your dealings. It's as simple as asking yourself how you go about *thanking* your customers. And not just for purchasing something, but also for reading your email, visiting your store, responding to your direct-mail piece, everything! This is *not* rocket science.

So how do I get my people to embrace these concepts? To live these brand principles?

The same way you get *customers* to respond to your brand. First, by appealing to what matters most to them, which is *them*—their lives, their families, their futures.

Start by covering the table stakes in your competitive environment: things like fair wages and benefits, an emotionally healthy work environment, fairness and transparency in your dealings with them, control over their own work, and recognition for achievement. Then provide opportunities for learning and growth.

But we can't provide all of that unless we start to grow.

It's a Catch-22, isn't it? That's why growth through innovation is the imperative. It's a virtuous cycle. Growth leads to more opportunities, higher morale, and enhanced communication, which in turn gets everyone passionate about the brand. You can't simply ask people to change—to work better together—and to expect it to happen. They have to want to, as well as know why and how. So put the brand—the business strategy—in their hands, and it will become impossible for them not to become engaged and to take responsibility.

Six: Innovation is the Key

"Sell your cleverness and purchase bewilderment."

Rumi

Tom: Well, it looks like we've started our descent. It really has been a pleasure.

Executive: *For me too Tom, thanks. But one last thing. You said "growth through innovation?" Do you mean new products?*

In some cases, but I'm referring to a *mindset* that continuously and creatively generates value for customers, and growth in revenue and profits for the organization.

The basic tendency of all systems is to dissipate energy in the absence of energy input. Innovation is your brand's energy input. It infuses energy both in the organization and in your audience.

It provides meaning.

Right. Beyond the mere numbers. It's funny. Companies are increasingly claiming that their cost structures are rising and their margins shrinking. This is true for most industries: consumer products, financial services, information technology, business-to-business, even not-for-profit. But in the face of this madness, they continue to benchmark their competitors and make incremental changes.

What madness?

What?

You said, "in the face of this madness?" What madness?

Mysteries, models, methods, madness

Rising costs and shrinking profits, caused by the refinement of methods to the point of marketplace indifference. Think about it this way. Since the beginning of business creation, successful brands have cycled through three phases of evolution: mystery, model, and method. Mystery is the "I wonder . . . ?" phase: *"I wonder if people will purchase an automobile if I can get the price down to 'x'?"* The next phase is the model phase, a messy, imperfect process: *"Let me try to produce an automobile for 'x.'"* Once the model phase has proven out the mystery—*"Wow! They will buy it."*—successful brands quickly move into the methods phase: *"How can I produce enough automobiles at the target price to fulfill demand, and make a profit while doing so?"* Some like Henry Ford are driven by insights regarding a market opportunity, while others are simply trying to stay ahead of the competition and remain profitable. Either way, a brand is born.

And then madness kicks in?

Settles in would be a more appropriate description. Henry Ford was guilty of this type of madness in his day. He was so convinced that his low-cost, mass production method *caused* the masses to buy his automobiles, that he was blinded by hubris to the mysteries of the changing marketplace. Do you remember Henry's response to multiple requests for a different color car?

"You can have any color you want as long as it's black?"

Exactly. Because black was an integral part of his refined method. Black paint dried faster than other paint colors, which enabled Henry to keep his manufacturing costs—and market price—where he believed they had to be to *cause* people to buy.

And that was Ford's madness phase?

One of them, but probably the biggest. Because what happened next? Alfred Sloan and General Motors entered the picture. While Ford continued to incrementally improve his scientific manufacturing methods, GM vigilantly mulled over a new customer mystery: *"I wonder if customers will pay more for a red or blue automobile?"* The answer was a resounding *"Yes"* and after implementing the methods to profitably support that answer—*"a car for every purse and purpose"*—GM rapidly rose to become Ford's archrival. Now this *is* a simplified version of historical events, but you can see this pattern played out over and over again in the annals of brand evolution. Go back again to the heydays of mass marketing, when customers dreamed of the "good life" and companies fulfilled those dreams with a wave of new products and services.

Days when we bought just about everything advertisers told us to buy.

That's true, and the media helped with universal stories about people owning a home in the suburbs with all the latest appliances, driving the latest model car, going out to restaurants and shows, etc. During that time models were being developed to answer all kinds of mysteries. Mysteries like: *"I wonder what people want to eat and how they want to eat it?"* One successful answer to *that* particular mystery was the McDonald brothers' *model* in California. But rather than take their discoveries and evolve their model into a large, profit-making *method*, Dick and Mac let Ray Kroc do it. Kroc figured out the expansion method, including exactly how long to cook a hamburger, exactly how to hire people, exactly how to set up and manage stores, and a brand was born. And what has happened to the once great McDonald's brand in the U.S. since the mid-'50s?

Madness?

Right. They've skillfully refined their method to the point of mediocrity *and* customer indifference. Although recently they've seemed to become aware of the madness of their ways.

But Tom, a lot of restaurant concepts become stale.

A lot of *business* concepts become stale. That's what I'm talking about. Think back to the mid 1990s. While the market leader, Motorola, was busy refining its methods to get to a few defects per million opportunities in its cell phone manufacturing process, a Finnish company, Nokia, with virtually no technology marketing expertise in the U.S. was answering a new customer mystery: *"I wonder if people will buy cell phones if they look more like fashion accessories."* That upstart not only answered the question and scaled the method, but it has gone on to become one of the world's dominant brands in digital technologies. Are you beginning to see the pattern?

I think so.

All 20th century brand successes evolved from mystery to method, and many have since moved into and—if they're smart and lucky—out of the madness phase: from Henry Ford with the assembly line to Sears with its retail method, to the legacy airlines with the madness of their high-cost methods.

And we prevent madness from settling in by . . . ?

Curiosity prevents arrogance

By not becoming arrogant. By staying curious and trying new things. Take a look at Howard Schultz's "method" called Starbucks, which scaled the affirmative answer to the mystery he conceived on a business trip—*"I wonder if people in Seattle will buy coffee from a Milan-inspired espresso bar?"* Starbucks continues to enhance its audience's hip, relaxed experience with new products like sandwiches, carbonated beverages, books and magazines, board games, even music downloads. Have all of Starbucks' "models" been successful? Of course not. But, that's the nature of the game.

We're living in an unprecedented time of marketplace mysteries, albeit not quite as obvious at the early 20th century: *"I wonder how people want to buy music? I wonder what people want to watch on television? I wonder how people want to interact with advertising? I wonder what people want to listen to on free radio? I wonder how people want to purchase financial services? I wonder . . . ?"* But instead of developing models to explore the mysteries, most established brands are moving into the madness phase as they place more and more emphasis and pressure on their worn-out methods. Successful brands will continue to come and go, but the great ones will discover answers to—and methods to leverage—the new marketplace mysteries of their times.

But don't organizations risk diluting their brands' equity by expanding into unrelated products and services?

Unrelated to what?

To their core competency. To what they are known and respected for.

First of all, a brand's "equity" is based on some *future* expectation: an expectation of the brand to deliver something of extraordinary value—something worth paying a premium for or telling their friends about *tomorrow*! But that's *someday*. Good luck trying to hold onto, predict, or "monetize" that scenario. It's futile. Leave it to the analysts. And a brand's core competency, its know-how? It should revolve around the collective consciousness of its audience—especially where it's headed—and *not* around the brand's legacy. What you're really asking about are the limits of so-called brand extension or brand "stretch."

Brand stretch?

I'm not sure of the origin of the phrase but it refers to a brand venturing into new products and services—like Apple's push into digital music. Maybe it's analogous to stretching the *fabric* of the brand, like spandex. You know, just because you *can* wear it, doesn't mean that you *should*.

[Exec laughs] *I've seen a lot of brand extensions lately. Heck, I own a pair of Caterpillar shoes.*

My neighbor owns a Jeep baby stroller. And why are we seeing this? Because companies are finally realizing that their most powerful assets are not their buildings, bank accounts, or even technologies. It's their relationship with their audience. The problems arise when a brand tries to be *all* things to *all* people. Instead, develop a core attitude with your core audience and be as many things as possible to *them*. And by "core" attitude, I mean the *real* you.

And what's the real us?

The genuine you. Remember, brands have personalities just like people, and we like to hang around with those that are smart, passionate, flawed, fun, and—most importantly in this world increasingly filled with staged experiences—authentic!

From core competence to core attitude

A core attitude instead of a core competency. It sounds interesting, but I don't know.

It's more than interesting; it's unique and compelling. Conventional brand wisdom resists most attempts to develop a business concept around an attitude. *"We need a defensible position. We need to own a space in the customer's mind."* Right? Unfortunately, that's why more than half of the businesses on the Fortune 500 list when I was in college are no longer in business. Face it, new and improved products and services will continue to appear at a mind-numbing rate due to today's unprecedented access to information and capital, and to emerging global markets. So the future of branding is to co-create with—and for—a passionate subculture of like-minded people. Discover their new mysteries. Lead them and educate them to new value propositions, new possibilities. But let me warn you. If you think you can use the strength of your relationship—your brand "equity"—as a launching pad for commonplace products and services, or ones that are new and cool but not compellingly relevant, you're nuts. People feel no sense of sentimental loyalty to you or your stuff. If your offering isn't of superior value, they won't even give it a second look.

One of the harsh realities of the marketplace, I guess. So how do we discover these mysteries?

One way is through open and honest dialogue, like we discussed earlier. Another is to be immersed in the culture, so that you have access to real-world information. *Immersed*, so you can do some *problem-finding. Immersed*, so you can stay attuned to how customers actually use your brand—their own organic innovations—and where you can discover how to link existing marketplace technologies and techniques to your audience's problems.

Another way is to simply listen to your own feelings. I love the story about Masura Ibuka approaching Akio Morita, founder of Sony, with his "idea" for the Walkman. He didn't sense some big, unfulfilled desire in the marketplace. He simply requested to put headphones on a portable tape player so that he could listen to his music without disturbing the people around him.

Empathy.

Right, com-passion. Com—"to connect with." Passion —"suffering." Turn your focus outward to those around you. Or simply be curious about things. John Vaught at HP saw a hot soldering iron touch a syringe and ink spurt out. So did he wipe it up? Of course not. He pulled out a high-speed camera to learn what had just happened. The result of his childlike curiosity was thermal inkjet printing.

That's cool. Let me ask you something. Earlier you made a somewhat derogatory remark about benchmarking. What's your problem with it?

If it's done to measure yourself against customer expectations, nothing at all. For example, if you have a website and you benchmark how quickly it loads against Amazon.com, because you know that people are using Amazon's site as a de facto standard for the way *all* websites—including yours—should present themselves, that's great! You're benchmarking against an expectation. On the other hand, if you're tweaking things that customers don't give a hoot about, you're wasting time and money. Stop slicing the baloney and hitting people with marketing come-ons, and get to work doing something special. Something that they truly care about.

Like what?

Exchange creates change

I have no idea, because I'm not part of your audience's "world." I'm not experiencing their dreams and problems, and I'm certainly not close enough to sense what's changing in that world. One of the biggest challenges in today's marketplace is the ability to *notice* change, because we all like to mentally grasp for security and predictability. We all resist changing the way we look at the world. But we must, because every new marketplace exchange creates some kind of cultural change, which in turn creates more marketplace exchange.

Exchange creates change. Change in what, precisely?

Most importantly, a change in expectations. Before Amazon.com people *expected* websites to load fairly slowly and to require multiple screens to place an order. Not any longer. Prior to nursing homes, people *expected* to care for their elderly family members in their homes. Not now. Prior to Apple people *expected* computers to be boring gray boxes. Now they're fashion statements. Marketing and innovation change brands whether a brand does anything to change itself or not. Do you see what I mean?

Yes, I think so. So then if we're part of our audience's world, if we're engaged with them, we'll be able to stay on top of their changing expectations, which may have been created through their interaction with others in the marketplace.

Exactly, or from their exposure to media influences or new technologies. Here, think of it this way.

[Exec smiles] *The pen?*

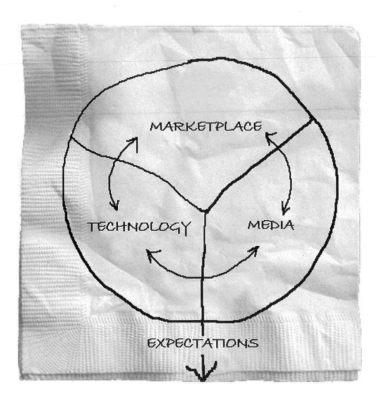

[Tom smiles] Thanks again. We're living in a culturally diverse marketplace buzzing with pleasure–seeking customers looking for the next best thing. And they're being relentlessly subjected to marketplace offerings, media influences, and new technologies. It's relatively simple for people to drop one thing, and pick and choose a new one to enhance one of their "worlds."

The marketplace is like one of those little cardboard toys where you spin various segments to create different faces. There are no average customers anymore like there were 40 or 50 years ago. People rebel against being like the Joneses. Instead, they want to spin that marketplace toy and become unique and special.

They go where their feelings take them.

Exactly. There are millions of people flitting in and out of thousands of little worlds or subcultures, and they are getting their information from an ever-growing number of communication channels: free TV, cable-TV, newspapers, radio, the Internet, their cell phones, video games, even highly specialized magazines. Do you realize, for example, that there are over 6 million readers of tuner magazines?

What's a "tuner?"

That's what *I* said. It's a person who gets-off on "souping up" his car.

Six million? Wow!

I know. You see, people continue to grow and specialize, building on new information and past experiences. So you have to stay on top of all of that mental activity and be a player in their "world"—the one in which you want to be relevant and important. And if you're quick to recognize and respond to changes, you'll be able to develop innovative offerings that will allow *you* to set your audience's expectations. You'll be creating demand, instead of fighting over it with others. Make it a priority of every member of your management team to discover those changes. Take a look at this.

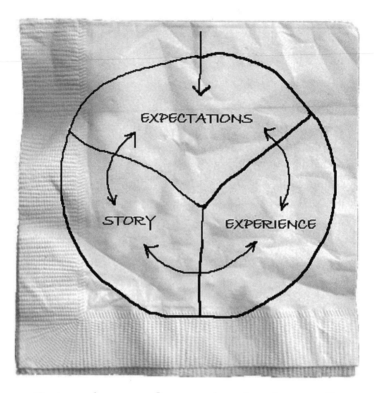

Once you have your finger on the pulse of your audience's changing expectations—which are driven by changes in the media, marketplace, and technology—refocus your people's priority to stimulating those expectations with compelling experiences and through the stories you tell in your advertising and other forms of communication.

Advertising, huh? So, we've come full circle on our branding conversation. You obviously don't believe in the "end of advertising" like some others. Do you mind discussing your thoughts on the subject for a minute?

Advertising will always be

Sure. I don't believe in the end of much of anything. And I'm sure that advertising will never go away, though it will change dramatically. What do you want to know?

Well, you've done a good job of highlighting the awesome amount of new marketplace offerings, as well as the fragmentation of media. So, how are brands supposed to "cut through" all of that noise?

First, go back to our first napkin chart and remember that it's about relevance first and foremost.

I understand that.

So you're asking me how to get the message out once you've discovered your audience's desires and habits, and developed something valuable and compelling?

Okay, sure. So how do we let them know about it?

[Tom smiles] I can't help it. Everyone thinks that market-place success comes down to "getting the message out," but take a look around. The marketplace is flooded with messages for stuff that nobody wants or cares about. And think about this. You don't see a lot of ads for Barnes & Noble, Starbucks, Ikea, or Urban Outfitter, but you *do* see a lot of people standing in line at their cash registers. Why? Because they create emotionally charged relationships with customers primarily through experiences with their products, retail environments, and face-to-face interactions.

So where does advertising fit into all of this?

Again, another subject that could fill an entire book. But okay, your communication is an integral part of how an audience views your brand. So whether it's an ad, a custom publication or cable program, a newsletter, or even a sales visit, remember to be relevant, communicate with your audience in context and on their terms, and for heaven's sake, try not to bore them.

Business relationships are like personal relationships. Attraction is the key. Being intellectually, socially, and emotionally engaging opens the door. Kindness, laughter, and fun keep the door open. And honesty, caring, and passion close the door with the brand and its audience on the same side.

So should we be trying to convey those attributes in all of our ads?

Advertising can't be reduced to a formula. It really depends. For example, if you want to entice people to experience your unique and highly relevant *new* product or service so that you can kick-off or deepen your relationship with them, a simple, brand-appropriate announcement may be a good way to go. Or perhaps sampling at a cultural event, or even a direct-mail or email promotion. Just make sure to be sensitive to how, where, and when your audience prefers to receive your communication. And be fun and informative. Project strength and energy in a crisp and catchy way.

But listen, if you're trying to foster a sense of community, shared experience and an attractive group identity on a deeper level, the important question to ask is not, *"What should the ad convey?"* Rather it's, *"What is the best way to communicate and interact with my audience to nurture these stronger ties?"* And to be sure, in that regard, advertising will remain a very powerful brand enhancer for many kinds of products.

What kinds of products?

Typically, commodity products and ones which influence how customers think about themselves when "using" them—like beer and liquors, perfume and cosmetics, jewelry and watches, cars, food, and fashion. People are not only consuming and wearing those products; they're also consuming and wearing the advertising—the brand stories.

Look. We know that advertising can help create expectations, and in the cases of these "cultural" products the expectations are a particular feeling about oneself realized through the experience with the brand story. It's the story that connects people emotionally with the brand. Stories that communicate, *"You're like us. You're right to think or act the way you do. We have the same sense of purpose, sense of humor, sense of others, and sense of self."* Do you see?

Sure, like Apple's cool iPod ads.

Right. Passionate customers want their brands to become a form of self-expression. They want to see themselves and their situation in a fun and surprising way. So when Apple runs artistically stunning ads or ones with the likenesses of Einstein, Picasso, and Gandhi imploring its audience to "Think Different," it helps the audience feel special. The brand advertising enhances their collective identity as artists and innovators who are changing the world.

What about ads as entertainment? Like Super Bowl ads or some of those viral Internet sites?

A lot of it is just attention-grabbing nonsense. They may be effective in getting people to chat up the brand to their buddies, but if the expectation is lacking—whether tangible or intangible—it will do little to build real value. Instead, brand owners should make sure the ad is associated with something meaningful to their audience —something that improves their lives, supports their cause, or provides identity value. There's no doubt that the line between advertising and entertainment is blurring, but developing the right message still revolves around the brand's strategy for growth.

I've read recently that a lot of people are more turned off to advertising than ever before. Is that right?

That's true. But it has more to do with the frequency, ubiquity, and mind-numbing repetitive nature of the advertising. See for yourself. Try to get a hold on why people are critical of *your* message. You'll find it may be because you're treating every interaction with them as an opportunity to get your message out, instead of as an opportunity to improve their lives. Or you may find you're communicating to them in an inappropriate way—condescending, dumbed-down, or just plain old annoying.

Branding is a dance. Yes, we like the reassurance of a familiar face, but we also want to be surprised and to laugh. Yes, we want order, but we also want some randomness—an adventure. Yes, we love excitement, but we also crave quiet time. Everything that touches our senses —especially those things we love the most, like music— is an alternation of stimuli: on, off, on, off, on, off. Your communication should be similar. Tickle their minds and their hearts. Don't smother them to death. As the philosopher Alan Watts once said, *"If you put your hand on the knee of a beautiful woman and leave it there, she'll cease to notice it. But if you gently pat her on the knee, she'll know you're still there. Because you come and you go. Now you see me, now you don't."*

[Exec laughs] *Well, I guess it may be time for us to lighten up a little and try some new things.*

There's an old Zen maxim, *"You can't control the waves, but you can learn to surf!"* We're living in a new world now

—one that revolves around the rapidly changing expectations of the customer. There's no stability. None. You must move with people, like a life preserver in a shifting sea. You must catch their wave. Get out there and interact with your audience. Find new and compelling ways to become meaningful to them. Try something new and see if it takes hold. You can't build a great brand by avoiding risks.

Be obsessed with the question.

With these *three* questions: What expected feeling will attract people to my brand and how best do we communicate it? What expected feeling will keep them engaged with us and how best do we deliver it? And what expected feeling will draw them away from us and how best do we discover it? Throw away the branding textbook. Forget about trying to engineer your brand. Instead, stay tuned in and connected to the living, breathing marketplace of your audience's fears, challenges, and aspirations. Find ways to cultivate and encourage those feelings that spontaneously arise. Branding is a journey, not a destination. Brand is a verb, not a noun.

[Flight attendant over intercom] "Thank you for flying with us. We know that you have a choice of many bankrupt airlines. And remember, no one values your money as much as we do."

[Tom smiles] Ahh . . . authenticity.

[Exec smiles] *And a dash of self-effacing humor. You can't beat it. Thanks again Tom. I really appreciate it.*

Thank you. And let me leave you with this G.K. Chesterton thought, *"There is a road from the eye to the heart that does not go through the intellect."* Great brands will pave *that* road and will leave the business of controlling and convincing people to the also-rans. Good luck and stay passionate!

"Change will lead to insight far more often than insight will lead to change."

Milton H. Erickson

Afterword

Creating an enduring brand is a huge challenge in today's rapidly evolving marketplace. It's similar to raising a child: it requires focused attention, intuition, and a lot of patience. It also requires a desire to change and adapt. Our natural instinct, however, is to shelter our brands, like our children, from the knocks and bumps that come in life. We want to keep our arms around them, keep them safe and under our control. But for children and brands to thrive in today's world, they must grow. We must encourage them to try new things, trip and fall, learn the hard lessons, find out what works and what doesn't, and be exposed to a variety of outside perspectives and truths.

The culture of the world is different today than it was years ago, just like raising a child today is different than it was years ago. And although we are exposed to a dizzying amount of opinions and techniques, the best way to address the complex job of brand-rearing is to recognize that, like raising a child, raising a brand takes a village. And that village is the complex web of relationships among your people, your customers, your partners, and other stakeholders. So teach your brand to be compassionate, authentic, appreciative, respectful, and, by all means, vibrant and alive. And if there is ever any way that I can help you during your journey, please don't hesitate to ask. I wish you well in your pursuits.

About the Author

Tom Asacker is a corporate advisor and an internationally acclaimed speaker. He is also the author of the popular business fable *Sandbox Wisdom* and *A Brand New World*, a Successories, Inc. leadership handbook.

Beyond his success as a writer and speaker, Tom is also a former corporate executive and an accomplished entrepreneur. He is the recipient of the George Land Innovator of the Year Award; holds medical patents and product design awards; and is recognized by *Inc.* Magazine, MIT, and the Young Entrepreneurs' Organization as a past member of their *Birthing of Giants* entrepreneurial executive leadership program.

Today, Tom helps professionals, companies, educational institutions, government agencies, and not-for-profit organizations transition from being economically driven to emotionally driven, so they can grow their brands by connecting deeply with their audience. Find out more about Tom and his philosophies by visiting www.acleareye.com.